The Gluten-free Cookbook for Kids

101 Exciting and Delicious Recipes

Adriana Rabinovich

Vermilion
LONDON

Dedication

This book is for Ruthie, my gorgeous gluten-free girl.
I love you so much

Contents

Introduction

Welcome to the wonderful world of gluten-free cooking. If you are browsing through this book, chances are you are looking for some help finding delicious, child-friendly meals for the gluten-free person in your life. You've come to the right place.

In this book you will find 101 tried-and-tested recipes for mouth-watering gluten-free meals. Birthday cakes, pancakes, sticky ribs, pizza, crispy chicken nuggets, soups, salads, brownies and chocolate chip cookies are just some of the 'forbidden foods' your child will now be able to enjoy.

Quick and easy to prepare, using readily available ingredients, these recipes will inspire you to prepare gluten-free food for the whole family, covering every eventuality from breakfast, lunch and tea to kids' favourites and party food. Most importantly, with these recipes your child will be able to enjoy life to the full, eating the sort of food that their non-gluten-free friends will clamour for.

A diagnosis of gluten intolerance requires a significant lifestyle change. To help you and your child cope with living gluten-free, I have included practical strategies, answers to frequently-asked questions and some creative advice on how to manage potentially tricky situations like eating out, school, holidays and birthday parties, as well as getting support from family and friends. There are even ideas on what to pack in your child's lunch box and a menu planner to make your day-to-day life easier (see pages 129, 214 and 215).

Ruthie – My inspiration

My primary objective in writing this book is to reassure you that following a gluten-free diet will not prevent your child from eating and enjoying delicious everyday food. I say this not as a casual bystander, but as someone who has experienced first hand what you may be experiencing at this very moment.

My daughter, Ruthie, was diagnosed with coeliac disease in December 2004 when she was 17 months. We returned home from the hospital feeling exhausted but so relieved to finally know what was wrong with our little girl. At the time she weighed less than 6kg (13lb) and had little or no energy to do the things most toddlers of her age were doing.

She became ill when we were on holiday and it took almost two months to find out what was causing her to lose weight so dramatically. There were other symptoms too, like her clinginess and sleeping six to seven hours during the day, which should have alerted us that something was seriously wrong. As a first-time mother, I felt so guilty for not picking up on these symptoms earlier. I have to confess that I did not know anything about coeliac disease, nor did I know what 'gluten-free' meant.

We were sent home from the hospital with a list of foods to be excluded from her diet. This included anything containing wheat, barley, oats or rye. On paper this did not feel too bad, but reality soon hit home. Toast and porridge for breakfast were out. Pasta for lunch was out. Sausages for tea were out. These were everyday favourites for which I would need to find alternatives.

'Her transformation encouraged me to find new things to eat. I set about converting existing recipes. I did lots of research and started inventing my own gluten-free recipes.'

Just a little bit of research revealed just how pervasive gluten is in our everyday life. Gluten, a protein found in cereal grains, appears in not just the most obvious foodstuffs like bread, biscuits, pizza, pasta and cereal, but also in the majority of processed foods including sauces, dips, crisps, chocolate, sweets, ice cream and even pre-grated cheese!

The first few weeks were tough as we got to grips with the new diet. But perseverance and creativity paid off and we were encouraged by seeing how quickly our daughter improved. Within two weeks of being gluten-free, she was transformed. She stood in her cot for the first time. She took her first steps unaided. She started to interact more with other children and adults. She was more alert. We were amazed! Her transformation encouraged me to find new things to eat. I set about converting existing recipes. I did lots of research and started inventing my own gluten-free recipes.

A few years on and the picture is very different. Ruthie is a vibrant 5 year old, full of energy, confident and ready to tackle anything you put in front of her. It was Ruthie who suggested the idea of a gluten-free cookbook for children. And the moment she said it, I knew I had to do it.

I use this cookbook day in and day out, and I can honestly say I would be completely lost without it. Writing and researching the recipes has been a wonderful experience and I am delighted to have the opportunity of sharing the results with you.

Adriana Rabinovich

section 1

going
gluten-free

1
understanding what gluten-free means

If your child, or someone you know, has recently been diagnosed with gluten intolerance, or coeliac disease, then the reality of living a gluten-free lifestyle will be starting to dawn. To make the many changes ahead, it helps to understand the condition: what causes it; its symptoms; and how best to treat it. Then you can help your child, your family members, friends and others to understand the importance of a gluten-free diet, making your child's life happier and healthier.

Below I have summarised some of the questions and answers that you may face.

What is gluten?

- Gluten is a protein found in cereal grains such as wheat, barley, rye and to some extent in oats.
- Gluten is present in many commercial products such as breads, cakes, soups, sauces, crisps, processed meats (such as sausages), gravy, seasonings, soya sauce, sweets, drinks and most ready-made meals.

How do I know if my child is intolerant to gluten?

- Symptoms for gluten intolerance (see box) can vary widely and can be difficult to pinpoint. If you suspect your child is gluten intolerant you must discuss this with your doctor or GP.
- Your doctor or GP can arrange a blood test. This test is used to detect specific antibodies present in people with coeliac disease. People with coeliac disease are unable to eat gluten.
- If the blood test proves positive, your GP will refer you to a

General Symptoms in Children

These symptoms can mirror other conditions so it is imperative that you seek medical advice before making any changes to your child's diet.

- Poor growth or weight loss
- Irritability
- Severe diarrhoea or severe constipation
- Chronic fatigue and anaemia
- Swollen stomach and stomach pain
- Vomiting and nausea

gluten-free cookbook FOR KIDS

specialist, usually a gastroenterologist. The gastroenterologist will perform a gut biopsy or endoscopy. This is done in hospital and will confirm his/her diagnosis.

- Please note that allergy testing kits are not suitable for testing gluten intolerance nor should you make any attempt to self-diagnose your child. It is imperative that you seek medical advice before making any changes to your child's diet.
- It is also worth noting that being allergic to wheat or gluten is different from being gluten intolerant.

What is coeliac disease?

- Coeliac disease is an autoimmune disease which affects the body's digestive system.
- If you are a coeliac and you consume gluten, your body reacts by sending antibodies to attack the gluten protein in the lining of the small bowel causing inflammation and damaging the villi. This is known as an autoimmune disease, because essentially the body is attacking itself.
- Villi are fine hair-like structures in your digestive tract, which slow down the passage of food in the intestine and aid digestion. This process allows nutrients in food to be absorbed. When the villi are damaged, food ingested flows straight through the digestive tract without being digested. This means that most of the nutrients in the food you consume are not absorbed by the body.
- Because the symptoms often mirror other conditions, like irritable bowel syndrome or some stress-related illnesses, coeliac disease can be difficult to diagnose.

Why has my child developed coeliac disease?

- Coeliac disease can be inherited and is known to run in families. If you have coeliac disease there is also an increased risk of having other autoimmune diseases, including Type 1 diabetes.

What is the treatment?

- Long term, if left untreated, coeliac disease can lead to malnutrition, osteoporosis (weak and brittle bones) and, particularly worrying in children, stunted growth and development.
- There is no known cure for coeliac disease. The only way to treat the disease is to completely exclude gluten from the diet. In the majority of cases this is a lifelong situation.
- When you are first diagnosed you will be referred to a nutritionist who will advise you on what foods to avoid and how to change your diet. It is important to continue to exclude these foods, as consumption of gluten, *however small*, will trigger symptoms.

When will my child start to feel better?

- You should notice an improvement within a few weeks of starting a gluten-free diet. The body will repair itself over time and you will soon see the benefits of improved nutrition.

What does 'gluten-free' mean?

Gluten-free means excluding gluten from your diet completely. Ensuring your child follows a gluten-free diet can be very difficult. For many, this is not something they will grow out of – it's a lifelong condition that requires a complete change in diet. But more than just a diet, being gluten-free can have many social and psychological implications. In the following section 'Adapting to a Gluten-free Lifestyle', I have made suggestions for dealing with different situations and helping your child to live a normal life.

The great news is that a gluten-free diet doesn't need to be dull or boring, and more and more people are choosing a gluten-free lifestyle simply for the health benefits. Less reliance on processed food and more emphasis on fresh, natural food will in itself make for a healthier diet. The recipes in this book are a great start!

How many people are affected by this condition?

- Coeliac UK, the registered charity, estimates that 1 in 100 people in the UK are affected by coeliac disease.
- Over 10,000 new cases are diagnosed in the UK each year.
- Coeliac UK estimates that 1 in 8 people have been diagnosed.
- Coeliac UK estimates that 500,000 people in the UK are living with the disease undiagnosed.

"Wheat-free" does not mean "gluten-free." Wheat-free products may contain barley, oats or rye, all of which contain gluten.'

In the USA it is estimated that up to 3 million people are affected by gluten intolerance. 1 in 133 people in the US will have coeliac disease, although only 1 in 4,700 will be diagnosed.

In Australia, 1 in 100 people have coeliac disease. More than 80 per cent (or the equivalent of 200,000 people) are living with this disease undiagnosed.

For further information on coeliac disease and organisations offering help and advice, see page 218.

2

adapting to a gluten-free lifestyle

Imagine giving up bread, pasta, pizza, cakes, biscuits and all pre-prepared food for life. Imagine what this must feel like for a child or a teenager, when their friends are enjoying burgers and pizzas. You can help your child to live with their new diet by preparing them for different situations, giving them the vocabulary and knowledge to make the right choices, and being honest with their friends so that they have help and support at all times.

How do I manage a gluten-free diet?

It is relatively straightforward to implement a gluten-free diet at home but you will need to be prepared and plan ahead for the many situations that you will encounter outside the front door. There is so much to say on this subject, but I will stick to the three problematic areas that you are likely to encounter on a regular basis.

Eating out

There is still a lot of work to be done making gluten-free food available at restaurants, cafeterias, coffee bars and snack bars. With a few notable exceptions, it is hard work trying to explain to waiters and food managers what gluten-free means. The level of knowledge and understanding is woefully inadequate in the catering trade, but I believe more is being done to increase awareness and educate chefs and catering staff on what constitutes 'gluten-free'.

In the meantime here are some suggestions to help:

- Always seize control and take some snacks with you. If a restaurant manager complains, explain that your child is gluten intolerant.
- When looking for a suitable restaurant, select cuisines which tend to be less gluten reliant. These include Indian, Thai, Latin American and Mediterranean food where gluten is less prevalent.
- Avoid Chinese food and fast food chains. Chinese food depends heavily on the use of soy sauce, which contains gluten. Fast food chains are also heavily reliant on wheat and gluten-based products. Equally, establishments that use a lot of pre-packed catering supplies may have a hard time establishing whether or not their ingredients are gluten-free. Something as basic as pre-grated cheese on a jacket potato may contain wheat flour.

- The best alternative is to look for restaurants where you know the food is made predominantly from scratch and of a good quality. Talk to the chef and the staff and get to know them. Also, get to know your local eateries. Sometimes, people will really surprise you and will go out of their way to cater for your child, especially when they realise that you are likely to become a regular customer.

Top Five Tips for Eating Out

1 Do not leave anything to chance. If possible, phone ahead and talk directly with the manager or even better the chef.

2 Always ask the waiter or the chef what is in a particular dish and all of its components. If the chef doesn't know, then the dish is best avoided.

3 Be especially careful of any sauces, gravies, chips, salad dressings and puddings. Never assume that they are gluten-free.

4 Repeat your gluten-free request with every course. For example, when you order an ice cream (make sure you ask if it is gluten-free) remind the waiting staff not to put any biscuits or sprinkles on top.

5 If the restaurant has done a good job, ask your child to thank the chef. This may seem a bit twee, but it does help to reinforce the message to the kitchen that their efforts are appreciated.

Gluten-free friendly menus

When choosing from a menu it is best to go for simple meat and vegetable options. This means grilled meat, chicken, fish or seafood, without any sauces or gravy. Potato and rice dishes can be gluten-free, but you must always ask if there are any other ingredients in the dish which may contain gluten. For example, some chips will be coated with a wheat-based product or may be fried in the same oil as other dishes containing gluten. Fresh fruit or jelly-based desserts and puddings are also generally good choices.

The following list offers some suggestions for gluten-free menu items. You must still make sure all of the items listed below do not contain any ingredient which may include wheat, rye, oats or barley. If the staff are in any doubt, then it's best to avoid. Grandparents, babysitters, relatives and friends may also find this list helpful.

gluten-free cookbook FOR KIDS

Gluten-free Menu Items

Guacamole with tortilla chips – check both are gluten-free

Olives

Poppadums

Prawn crackers – check not fried in oil with other items containing gluten

Crudités (fresh raw vegetables) and hummous – check gluten-free

Prawn cocktail – check sauce is gluten-free

~☆~

Tuna salad with mayonnaise – check mayonnaise is gluten-free

Omelette with oven chips – check chips are gluten-free

Grilled or roasted chicken with mashed potatoes or roasted
potatoes – no gravy

Grilled or baked fish with buttered rice

Grilled steak with oven chips – check chips are gluten-free

Grilled chicken drumsticks

Roast meat (lamb, beef, chicken or pork) – check gravy is gluten-free

Rice dishes (paella, pillau, risotto)

Steamed vegetables

Corn

Baked potatoes with cheese and beans –
check beans and cheese are gluten-free

~☆~

Fresh fruit with cream

Sorbet or ice lollies

Jelly

Meringues

Rice pudding

Yoghurt – check gluten-free

Chocolate – check gluten-free

Cross-contamination

Cross-contamination will occur when any product or food containing gluten is in contact with a gluten-free product or food. It is imperative that cross-contamination is avoided, as even a very small amount of gluten (this could be flour dust or just a few breadcrumbs) can make a gluten intolerant person ill. Basic food hygiene in addition to some training in preparing food for people with allergies, is key to ensuring your child's health is not compromised.

Basic Rules for Avoiding Cross-contamination

1 If toasting bread, you must have a separate toaster for gluten-free bread.

2 Have separate chopping boards for gluten-free food – bread in particular.

3 Prepare gluten-free food in a specific area of the kitchen and make sure that the area is spotless before you begin preparing a gluten-free meal.

4 Never stir a gluten-free sauce or gluten-free pasta with the same spoon you have used to stir a sauce or pasta containing gluten – this is a very easy mistake to make! If you do make a mistake, you must throw away the sauce or pasta, wash all utensils and pots thoroughly and start again.

5 Make sure oven gloves, aprons and tea cloths are spotlessly clean before handling or preparing gluten-free food.

6 Gluten-free baked goods, cookies, breads, cakes, etc must be made in a dedicated facility away from products containing gluten.

7 Products which appear to be gluten-free, but have been made in a facility which handles gluten will carry a high risk of cross-contamination and should be avoided.

8 Never put gluten-free biscuits or bread in the same container as biscuits or bread containing gluten. This also means having dedicated lunch boxes, drinks bottles, food containers for gluten-free products.

Travelling and holidays

Airports and motorway restaurants are notorious black spots for gluten-free food. My advice is to bring a range of snacks with you. If you order a gluten-free meal on your flight, it's still a good idea to carry some extra provisions with you. Sometimes airline catering is not very reliable and the special meal you ordered may not actually materialise. On a short haul journey you will be able to manage but on a long haul flight you really do need a back-up plan.

'It's worth doing a bit of research before you book your holiday. Choose your country carefully. Italy, weirdly enough, is fantastic for gluten intolerant people.'

When travelling abroad as a family we've found the best solution is to stay in self-catering accommodation. This gives you the opportunity to prepare meals like breakfast and lunchtime picnics, leaving you with only one meal to eat out, if you feel like it. It definitely takes the pressure off knowing that there is less likelihood of your child getting ill and you can choose to eat out, when you find a restaurant that will cater for your child.
In some hotels it is also possible to request a mini fridge in your room. You can then go to a local shop and keep some basic supplies on hand.

Tuscan Toast

The idea originates from my brother-in-law Scotty. He used to make this for breakfast when we stayed in a very primitive house in Umbria, in Italy. It was inspired by the lack of a toaster and the fact that bread in Tuscany is made without salt. The result is really yummy and always reminds me of those glorious Italian holidays.

Gluten-free bread, sliced
Olive oil
Maldon sea salt

● In a heavy frying pan warm a very small amount of olive oil. Place the gluten-free bread in the pan and over a medium heat toast the bread until lightly coloured and crispy. Sprinkle with a little bit of salt and then flip over to toast the other side.
● Serve straight out of the pan.

ToAst

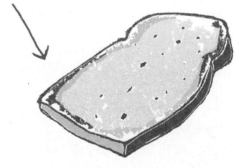

THIS SIMPLE RECIPE IS A REAL LIFE-SAVER WHEN TRAVELLING AS YOU DON'T NEED TO WORRY ABOUT CRUMBS FROM THE TOASTER CONTAMINATING YOUR GLUTEN-FREE BREAD.

'There is a really useful website www.glutenfreepassport.com which has free downloads of dining cards with translations in several languages.'

Suitcase Store Cupboard

Regardless of where you stay, here are a few handy things to pack in your suitcase:

A few packs of gluten-free pasta
A container with some gluten-free breakfast cereal
A few packs of gluten-free crackers, biscuits and snacks
A jar of peanut butter or Marmite
Some extra containers with lids. These are really useful if you find a good delicatessen or grocery store.

School

Inform the school of your child's special diet as soon as possible. Most schools are now catering for a large range of food intolerances and allergies so this should not be too much of a problem. Give the school as much notice as possible and put your request in writing. Speak to the person in charge of catering and discuss your concerns, particularly issues regarding cross-contamination.

There is a standard letter available from Coeliac UK (see page 218), which you can send to your child's school. I used this as a starting point but also asked that where possible, I would prefer for my child to be offered a similar gluten-free alternative. Of course, this may not always be practical, but it is something you should try to encourage the school to do. It may help sharing with the catering team some straightforward recipes and pointing them in the direction of a useful website, so they can get an idea of what is possible. Sometimes people are more likely to say no when they feel overwhelmed and not fully aware of what gluten-free means. If you provide them with information and recipes, they may be more receptive.

It is also a good idea to make sure that your child's teachers are aware of the situation. They may need to monitor your child during break times, to ensure they are not swapping their snacks with other children. It is a good idea to send in a small container each term with some special biscuits or treats that the teacher can use at their discretion. If it's another child's birthday and they have brought sweets to share with the class, your child won't be left out.

For school outings and day trips it is best to provide your child with a packed lunch. Don't expect cafeterias in museums, zoos or other child-friendly establishments to have any gluten-free items on their menus because, frankly, most of the time they won't. For longer overnight trips, it may be worth speaking to the catering manager at the site. Pack a few gluten-free items in your child's suitcase just in case.

Finally, it is very important to discuss these issues with your child. Where possible allow them to control the situation by giving them the tools and knowledge to express themselves.

Banana

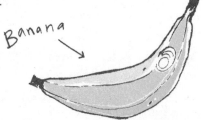

Gluten-Free Playdough

Many children at pre-school and in nurseries enjoy playing with stretchy playdough. As normal playdough is made with wheat, I have included a recipe for a gluten-free version:

300g (2 cups) gluten-free flour
140g (½ cup) salt
45g (¼ cup) cream of tartar
420ml (2 cups) water

2 tbsp vegetable oil
Food colouring (optional)
Vanilla/almond extract

● In a large saucepan mix all the ingredients together with a whisk and mix until lump free. Cook over a medium heat for about 2 minutes, stirring constantly until the mixture starts to firm up. Allow to cool and knead for a few minutes to help get rid of any remaining lumps. The mixture may be a bit sticky, if so, add a little more oil as you're kneading it. Allow the playdough to sit for a few hours as this may help to make it less goey.
● This will keep in an airtight container or in a plastic bag for a few weeks.

Note: The amount of salt stated is not an error! It will stop little ones eating the dough as it will taste really horrible.

ONCE YOU ARE READY TO USE YOUR PLAYDOUGH, YOU CAN USE THE FOLLOWING ITEMS TO MAKE IT EVEN MORE FUN!
GLITTER
SPICES (STAR ANISE AND CINNAMON)
HERBS FROM THE GARDEN (ROSEMARY AND LAVENDER)
FLOWERS AND FLOWER PETALS

cupcakes

3

getting help along the way

Much of helping your child to adapt to a gluten-free lifestyle will be in learning to accept their new diet. Enlisting the help of your family, your child's friends and their parents or carers, will ensure that everyone understands what gluten-free means and help to smooth the way.

How can I help my child with their new diet?

I personally feel it is important for all the family to eat the same meals at home where possible. This sends a clear message to everyone in the household that you are united in helping your child stick to their diet. If your child is constantly surrounded by tempting foods, it will be much harder to ensure they are staying gluten-free.

Of course, it is not realistic to expect siblings or other adults in the family to follow a strict gluten-free diet all the time but the logistics of cooking different meals for different members of the family is something I would try to avoid.

If you find it impossible to completely exclude gluten from your home (and it is very difficult) then try to limit what is allowed. Keep any items containing gluten in a separate cupboard or basket and make sure you label any items in the fridge clearly. Be extra careful with pots of jams and butter, because any residual crumbs can cause a gluten reaction. Likewise, shared drinks bottles or cups can be a source of cross-contamination.

'Some children are extremely sensitive to gluten and a few crumbs unwittingly consumed can make them ill.'

There is no way of denying that there is a psychological component surrounding children who need to follow a special diet. This is a delicate subject, which only you as a parent will be able to judge. The age of the child when diagnosed will have a big effect on how they will cope with the restrictions. It is safe to say that the older the child, the more likely you are to meet resistance. Younger children are more pliable and you are likely to have more control over their diet. Much of the research indicates that as children get older the temptation to break the diet increases. That's why you need to get good habits ingrained from a young age, so that eating gluten-free becomes completely natural.

Coeliac UK publish an annual Food and Drink Directory which lists over 10,000 products which are gluten-free. Products are listed by manufacturer and brand name and there are also entries for retailers own brands. This is an invaluable resource. Copies are free to members of Coeliac UK. For further copies or more information you can contact them on www.coeliac.org.uk.

Foods to Avoid – What's In, What's Out

Out	In
Pasta	Rice noodles, gluten-free pasta, potatoes, corn
Pizza	Cheese on gluten-free toast, cheese nachos/tacos with tomato salsa
Sausages	Gluten-free sausages, chicken wings, chicken drumsticks, bacon strips, ham, turkey
Bread	Rice cakes, gluten-free crackers or gluten-free breadsticks
Biscuits	gluten-free biscuits, meringues, chocolate, marshmallows, fresh fruit
Cake	Jelly, sorbet, yoghurt, chocolate mousse
Crisps	gluten-free pretzels, poppadums, prawn crackers, popcorn, raw veggies

Please check all ingredient labels carefully to ensure foods suggested are gluten-free.

Family and friends

How you handle siblings and friends will depend to a large extent on your child's character. Do not underestimate the power of peer pressure. If appropriate, use this to your advantage and as a way of helping your child.

My advice is to have an open conversation with all the key people who have daily contact with your child. Let your child participate in these conversations and allow everyone the opportunity to ask questions. Grandparents, child minders, au pairs, friends and family can actually help. The more they understand why your child can't eat certain foods the more they will be able to support your child.

When your child reaches the age where they are able to go on play dates or for tea after school, it will help them if you can discuss their requirements openly with the parent or carer who will be catering for them. Your child needs to feel confident that they will be able to socialise with their friends and enjoy meals, without getting ill.

Gingerbread

Gluten-free Play Dates

Here are a few tips when discussing a gluten-free play date with parents or carers:

- Discuss the importance of ensuring that all ingredients are gluten-free and the risks of cross-contamination.

- Suggest recipes or brands of food that are safe.

- Provide a packet of gluten-free pasta so that everyone can eat the same dish.

- Provide snacks for your child in case they can't eat what is on offer.

- For a sleepover, send your child with suitable breakfast food, too.

Fussy eaters

It is not surprising that a child with coeliac disease may be a fussy eater. Food may have been a source of great pain and discomfort for many months and sometimes years before they have been diagnosed. What can you do? Be patient. Do not make your child eat anything they don't want to eat and do not make mealtimes a battleground. Keep offering alternatives. Keep trying new things. Don't give up. And if you run out of ideas and are pulling your hair out then a few more suggestions follow:

☆ Keep portion sizes small. Start with a tiny bit. If they like it and want more, that's a great start.
☆ Encourage your child to taste new things, but never force them. Make it a game.

☆ Make mealtimes exciting. Change the venue. Serve breakfast outside or under the stairs. Serve tea in the playroom or somewhere totally unexpected.

☆ Change the cutlery: give them chopsticks, a new plate, a new drinking cup.

☆ Take the emphasis off the food and place it on the ambience, play music, put up fairy lights, dress up, make it feel special.

☆ Turn the kitchen into a restaurant or café and let them order their food from a menu. This is a really good way for young children to learn what food they can eat and starts to give them the confidence to express themselves and cope with difficult situations.

☆ Pretend you are the one with a special diet and they are the chef or waiter. Ask if they have anything gluten-free on the menu you can eat.

☆ Let your children choose what to have for tea every once in a while. It's amazing to see how once you start giving your child some control over the situation, how quickly they will start to feel better about what choices are available to them.

☆ You will have good food days and bad food days. Try not to beat yourself up about it. Listen to your child, respect their feelings and learn from them everyday.

Avocados

Carrots

Broccoli

Birthday parties

Parties tend to magnify what children can't eat and that is why it is so important to find ways to help your child cope in these situations.

Birthday Party Coping Tips

Here are a few tips:

☆ Talk to your child. Be open and upfront about the party they will be attending and tell them what to expect. Don't hide things from them.

☆ For very young children it's important you do this each time you go to a party (usually in the car!) so they get used to the drill. Get them to play it back to you as well, so you are sure they have got it.

☆ Explain what foods they will be able to eat and what they must avoid. The more informed and knowledgeable they are about what they can't eat, the easier it will be for them to cope.

☆ Explain to their friends why your child can't eat gluten. Children are often more accepting and thoughtful than you might expect.

See pages 216 and 217 for some suggested gluten-free party menus.

Dealing with the person hosting the party presents its own set of problems. I often find this the most difficult part as it always feels a bit awkward asking someone to go out of their way to cater for my child's special diet, especially if you don't know them.

Tips for Dealing with Parents

- Phone the host at least a week before the party. Don't leave it until the last minute. Remember that if you phone too much in advance, they may actually forget!

- Explain that your child is gluten intolerant and what that means.

- Enquire, as nicely as you can, what she/he is planning to serve at the party. Ask if it is okay if you bring something gluten-free.

- Let the host know that you are happy to make or buy something similar to what will be on the menu and that you will bring enough to share with other children. This may sound over the top, but it will make your child feel like they are being included if they see other children eating gluten-free food, too.

- If time constraints prevent you from bringing food to the party, then another option is to bring a lunch box with some of your child's favourite food. If you are not staying at the party with your child this is by far the best solution. That way, there is less risk that your child will be offered something which they can't eat. Ask another parent at the party to keep an eye on your child.

- Feed your child before the party. A hungry child facing a table of lots of forbidden food is not a good idea.

The birthday cake

The birthday cake is my worst moment. It breaks my heart when my daughter says 'I can't eat that'.

I have tried lots of strategies, which have included leaving before the cake is presented and bringing along a home-made, gluten-free birthday cake to go alongside the 'real' birthday cake. That was truly over the top and completely backfired on me.

The best solution is to bring along a plate of Lovely Little Cupcakes (see page 198). You can keep a stash of these in the freezer ready to go. Most children love cupcakes (especially the icing) and if you have enough to go around everyone will be happy. It is best to let the host know a few days in advance that you will be bringing these, Bring them ready plated on paper plates and let the host present them at the appropriate time.

If cupcakes are not your thing, then there are lots of other easy party food recipes in this book you can select from (see page 193).

cupcakes

Eggs

Electric whisk

Lemon curd

4

a gluten-free kitchen

Gluten-free cooking doesn't require any specialist equipment but you will need to familiarise yourself with the 'free-from' isle at the supermarket and be very careful when selecting ingredients. Check the labels for food-stuffs containing wheat or wheat derivatives as well as other gluten additives. Here are a few pointers to help you get the most out of this cookbook and to help you select ingredients for delicious gluten-free meals.

What do I need to get started?

Below I have listed all the pieces of equipment that are required for preparing and cooking the recipes in this book. You will find many of them in your kitchen cupboards already and, if not, you will soon build a useful resource.

Scales (battery-operated
are best)
Measuring spoons
Measuring jug
Selection of wooden spoons
and spatulas
A set of mixing bowls
(small, medium, large)
Selection of baking tins
including:
- American style 12-hole
  muffin tin
- Mini muffin baking tin
- A square 23 cm (9in) tin
- A 500 g (1 lb) loaf tin
- 2 round 20 cm (8in) cake tins
- A large cake tin for
  celebration cakes

sieve

- Two baking sheets
- Two wire racks
Assorted cookie cutters
Rolling pin
Palette knife
Pastry brush
Large metal spoon
2 metal sieves (medium, small)
Silicone baking mats
Greaseproof paper
Parchment paper
Paper muffin cases
(normal size and mini)
Greaseproof paper liners
for loaf tins
Clingfilm
Aluminium foil

gluten-free cookbook FOR KIDS

Electric mixer

An electric mixer is a very useful bit of kit. A small hand mixer is fine and has the advantage of not taking up much space when it's not in use.

Hand-held blender

A hand blender is something that I confess I can no longer live without. I use mine almost every day to make soups, smoothies, dips, baby food and purées. It's much more portable than a liquidiser or food processor and easier to wash up.

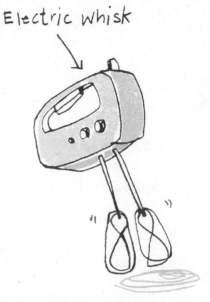

Electric whisk

Labels

Always check the ingredient labels, especially on spices and condiments. Gluten is often used as a thickener so it is present in lots of processed foods and ready-made meals. Manufacturers sometimes change recipes and plant procedures without warning. So, sometimes a brand you know to be gluten-free, suddenly isn't – always do a quick scan of the ingredients just in case. Remember a label stating 'wheat-free' does not mean 'gluten-free'.

Store cupboard ingredients

Here is a list of some the most commonly used ingredients in this book. The list may seem long but many of these will be in your cupboard already. Also, you don't need to start with everything on the list – build up your pantry as you go along.

Store Cupboard Ingredients

Flours and Grains
- Cornflour
- Quick cook polenta
- Buckwheat flour
- Basmati rice
- Arborio rice
- Brown rice
- Brown rice flakes
- Gluten-free cornflakes
- Gluten-free crispy rice
- Gluten-free bread

Dairy Products
- Milk (semi-skimmed or whole)
- Buttermilk
- Cream (double and single)
- Crème fraîche
- Soured cream
- Yoghurt (thick Greek yoghurt, natural yoghurt)
- Cheese (Cheddar, Gruyère, Parmesan)
- Soft cheese

Sugar and Sweeteners
- Caster sugar
- Light brown sugar
- Dark brown sugar
- Demerara sugar
- Icing sugar
- Honey
- Maple syrup
- Liquid glucose (or Karo Corn Syrup)

Seasonings and Condiments
- Pepper (black and white)
- Salt
- Concentrated liquid chicken stock
- Stock cubes
- Fresh organic chicken stock
- Gluten-free soy sauce (also known as Tamari Soy Sauce)
- Cinnamon

Many of these items are available at good supermarkets. See the list of suppliers on page 218, for those items not currently available in supermarkets.

- Nutmeg
- Chilli powder
- Curry powder
- Mustard powder
- Bay leaf
- Vanilla extract
- Gluten-free ketchup
- Gluten-free mayonnaise
- Olive oil
- Vinegar (white wine, red wine, cider, balsamic)
- Fresh herbs
- Garlic
- Onions
- Celery
- Ginger
- Lemons

Leavening Agents and Baking Ingredients

- Gluten-free plain flour
- Gluten-free baking powder
- bicarbonate of soda
- *Xanthan gum
- Chocolate chips
- Plain cooking chocolate

Nuts and Dried Fruit

- Ground almonds
- Hazelnuts
- Pecans
- Sesame seeds
- Dried cherries
- Dried cranberries
- Dates
- Raisins
- Apricots

*Currently available on prescription

Gluten-free pasta

Gluten-free pasta varies greatly. I avoid most corn-based pasta as this tends to have too strong a flavour and the texture is never quite right. However, Italian gluten-free pasta is the best and this does contain maize starch, made from corn.

Gluten-free flour

Gluten-free flour is readily available in good supermarkets and is a great way of cooking previously forbidden foods, such as cakes.

XANTHAN GUM IS A NATURAL INGREDIENT USED TO GIVE ELASTICITY AND TEXTURE TO GLUTEN-FREE FOODS. IT IS MOST OFTEN USED IN BAKED PRODUCTS. XANTHAN GUM IS AVAILABLE ON PRESCRIPTION BUT IT IS ALSO STOCKED IN MOST HEALTH FOOD SHOPS AND HAS RECENTLY BECOME AVAILABLE IN SUPERMARKETS.

A note on the recipes

The recipes in this cookbook have been developed for children of all ages and for grown-ups. This book is all about encouraging your children to get involved with the cooking. Many of the recipes are very forgiving and are suitable for cooking with your child. However, an adult must always supervise children in the kitchen.

Before you start cooking

Being organised and methodical in the kitchen will help speed things up and give you better results. I suggest you read through the recipe first, then weigh out and measure all the ingredients in the recipe before you start.

Seasoning

You may need to adjust the seasoning accordingly, for example for very young children, use less salt and spices, for older children and teenagers, you may want to increase the seasoning and up the heat a bit.

Nuts and honey

Please note that many of the recipes in this book contain nuts and are therefore not suitable for children with nut allergies. Also, very young children can choke on nuts. Therefore, where a recipe calls for chopped nuts or whole nuts please omit them (or substitute with something else) if you are making this for a baby or a child under 3. Also, babies under 1 year must not be given honey.

Butter

All of the recipes in this book have been tested using good-quality unsalted butter. This will give you the best results and allows you to add salt to your preference.

Eggs

The eggs used in all of the recipes are large, free-range and organic.

Salt

Maldon sea salt is my preferred seasoning. This is because it tastes great and you need less than normal table salt to get the same level of saltiness.

Gluten-free flour

All of the recipes in this book have been tested using commercially available plain white gluten-free flour.
Note: Gluten-free flour mixes available on prescription are not suitable for the recipes contained in this book.

Gluten-free pasta

When cooking gluten-free pasta always use lots of water, at least 1 litre (1¾ pints) of water per 100 g (4 oz) of pasta. Stir frequently as the pasta is cooking to prevent sticking.

Portions

For each recipe I have indicated how many the recipe will serve. This is generally based on two adults and two children under 10. If you've got hungry teenagers you may need to revise the quantities accordingly.

Oven temperatures

Cooking and baking times given in the recipes should be taken as a guide. Oven temperatures vary greatly from oven to oven and every oven has its own personality. This will have an effect on cooking times and on the final results. Get to know your oven and its quirks. If you feel a bit uneasy or unsure, the best way to check your oven is working to temperature is to invest in an oven thermometer.

Freezer

Many of the recipes in this book are suitable for freezing. Having a stash of ready-made food is a real bonus, especially as most ready-made supermarket meals are not gluten-free. Label things clearly with the date made and the number of portions. Discard anything that is more than 6 weeks old – it won't harm you but the taste and texture may be compromised after this time.

Note: To convert an existing recipe to gluten-free, first assess how critical the flour is to the texture of the product. For example, in bread, gluten gives the characteristic of chewiness and elasticity. I would therefore not attempt to convert a bread recipe as this is unlikely to work. For cakes and biscuits you can get very good results. In general, I would substitute half gluten-free flour and half ground almonds for normal flour. If making a cake, add 1 tsp of xanthan gum per 200g of flour as this will greatly improve the texture. Biscuits with a more cakey texture, will also benefit from a small amount of xanthan gum, about ½ – ¼ teaspoon. But don't overdo it. Too much will give you an unpleasant texture and aftertaste. When making crisp biscuits, reduce the liquid content a bit and add more chopped toasted nuts. This improves the texture and flavour. For sauces and gravies which use only a small amount of flour, you can substitute like for like.

Eggs

section 2

gluten-free recipes

top ten kids' favourites

This chapter contains a selection of classic kids' favourites, those childhood staples that are regularly served at tea time in every household. Many of these recipes are for previously 'forbidden' foods, such as pizza, fish fingers and chocolate cake, so they make a great starting place when entertaining your child's friends and when making the difficult transition to a new diet.

Shepherd's Pie SERVES 4–6

Always a favourite with children, Shepherd's Pie is a must in your gluten-free repertoire. It can be made in advance and it also freezes well if you happen to have any leftovers.

500 g (1 lb) minced lamb
2 garlic cloves, crushed
About 75 g (3 oz), tomato pureé
1 bay leaf
1 tsp dried thyme
A dash of gluten-free
concentrated chicken stock
Salt and pepper

FOR THE TOPPING
4 medium potatoes, peeled
and cut into chunks
Butter
Milk
Grated Parmesan cheese

● Put the minced lamb in a medium saucepan and cook on a high heat for several minutes, stirring with a wooden spoon. Most supermarket lamb will contain a fair amount of water and fat (the better quality the meat the less liquid and fat), which will start to appear in the saucepan. After cooking for about 5 minutes, drain the meat in a colander and get rid of the liquid. If you don't do this, you may end up with a very greasy and liquidy Shepherd's Pie.
● Place the meat back into the saucepan. Add the tomato purée to the lamb along with the crushed garlic. Continue to cook over a high heat for a few minutes, stirring to make sure the lamb doesn't burn. Now add enough water to cover the meat, plus a tiny bit extra. Add the bay leaf, thyme, salt and pepper to taste and a little dash of liquid chicken stock.

● Bring the heat down to simmer, cover and cook for 20–30 minutes checking and stirring every once in a while and adding a bit more water if necessary. Taste for seasoning and decant into an ovenproof dish. Allow to cool for at least 20 minutes before adding the topping.

● Pre-heat the oven to 180°C (350°F) Gas 4.

● To make the mashed potato topping, bring a large pan of water to the boil. Add the potatoes and cook until just soft. Drain and place them back in the pan. Add some milk and a generous chunk of butter, salt and pepper. Mash and add more butter and milk if necessary to make a soft but not runny mash. Season accordingly. Dollop the topping on to the meat mixture in the dish, making sure to cover the entire dish. Sprinkle generously with grated Parmesan. Bake in the oven for 20–30 minutes until the topping is golden and the lamb is bubbling.

IDEAL FOR THE FREEZER!

Crispy Chicken Nuggets

SERVES 6–8

(MAKES APPROX 30 NUGGETS)

These are a favourite for parties and I like to serve them with oven chips for a fun chicken 'n' chips night. These nuggets freeze very well, so you can make a batch for the freezer and use as and when required.

150 g (5 oz) gluten-free cornflakes
2 eggs
100 g (4 oz) gluten-free plain flour

4–6 chicken breasts, about 800 g
(1¾ lb), cut into chunks
Olive oil

● Place the cornflakes in a food processor and whiz until fine. Alternatively, put them in a plastic bag and crush them with a heavy object, such as a pan or a rolling pin.

● Put the eggs in a large bowl and beat lightly. Put the flour in another bowl and season with salt and pepper. Put the crushed cornflakes in a large bowl.

● Dredge the chunks of chicken in batches, first in the flour, then in the egg and finally in the cornflakes. Place on a baking sheet. Continue until you have used up all the chicken. You can freeze the nuggets at this point, or keep them in the fridge for up to one day.

● When you are ready to serve them, pre-heat your oven to 200°C (400°F) Gas 6. Drizzle the nuggets with olive oil and then put them in the oven for 10–15 minutes until golden. Check that they are cooked through before serving.

12345678910

IDEAL FOR THE FREEZER!

To freeze

Place the uncooked nuggets in a container using greaseproof paper between layers. They will keep in the freezer for about 1 month. To use these from frozen place them directly on a baking sheet and lightly drizzle with little olive oil. Place them in a hot oven for about 15-20 minutes until completely cooked through.

chicken nuggets

Deborah's Delicious Meatballs *SERVES 4–6*

I love meatballs, but often find they are time consuming and high maintenance. Not this recipe! I watched my friend, Deborah, make these and it took less then 5 minutes to get them in the oven.

2 slices gluten-free bread – including crusts!
100 ml (3½ fl oz) milk
1 tbsp olive oil
1 small onion, finely sliced
500 g (1 lb) organic minced pork

1 heaped tbsp gluten-free tomato ketchup
1 heaped tbsp mayonnaise
1 tbsp American-style gluten-free mustard
50 g (2 oz) mature Cheddar cheese, grated

● Pre-heat the oven to 180°C (350°F) Gas 4.
● Place the bread in a bowl and add the milk. Leave to soak for a few minutes and mash up. Meanwhile, heat the oil in a small frying pan and add the onion. Sauté for a few minutes until softened.
● Put the pork in a large bowl. Add the cooked onion, soaked bread, ketchup, mayonnaise, mustard and grated cheese. Mix together gently. Form into 12 large meatballs and place on a baking sheet. You can leave them in the fridge for a few hours or bake them straight away.
● Bake in a pre-heated oven for about 20–25 minutes. Serve immediately.

1 2 **3** 4 5 6 7 8 9 10

NOTE: TRY NOT TO OVERHANDLE THE MIXTURE WHEN MIXING THE INGREDIENTS TOGETHER — IT NEEDS TO BE DONE GENTLY WITH A LIGHT TOUCH.

MENU IDEA! DEBORAH'S MEATBALLS WITH ORGANIC BROWN RICE AND NAN'S CHOPPED SALAD (PAGE 122)

THE TEXTURE OF THESE MEATBALLS IS VERY GENTLE AND SOFT SO EVEN VERY YOUNG CHILDREN WILL LOVE THEM.

IDEAL FOR THE FREEZER!

Fish Fingers *(MAKES ABOUT 10 FISH FINGERS)*

Always a favourite with children, these fish fingers are so much nicer than the store-bought kind. They also freeze very well and you can put them straight in the oven from the freezer. Allow a little extra cooking time.

1 tbsp olive oil
Freshly squeezed juice of
½ lemon
300 g (10 oz) white fish, skinned
(such as cod, hake or halibut)
1 egg
2 tbsp milk
50 g (2 oz) seasoned cornflour
Melted butter

TOPPING
Select from one of the following:
75 g (3 oz) gluten-free cornflakes,
finely ground
75 g (3 oz) polenta
4–5 slices gluten-free bread,
toasted and made into
breadcrumbs (see over)

● Combine the olive oil and the lemon juice in a bowl. Add the fish and leave to marinate for 15–20 minutes. Combine the egg and milk in a bowl. Put the seasoned cornflour in a separate bowl. Select the topping you are using and place in another bowl. Line a baking sheet with greaseproof paper.

● Remove the fish from the marinade. Cut into chunks or fingers roughly the same size and thickness. Dip the chunks first in the seasoned cornflour, then in the egg and finally in the coating. Place on the baking sheet. Continue until all of the fish is used up.

● If you are cooking the fish fingers straight away, pre-heat the oven to 220°C (425°F) Gas 7. Drizzle each finger with a little melted

butter. Bake for 10–15 minutes depending on the thickness of the fingers. Serve immediately with ketchup or with Soft Cheese Herb Dip (see page 195).

To freeze
Place in a container with sheets of greaseproof paper in between layers. Seal tightly. They will keep for 1 month in the freezer.

To make breadcrumbs
Toast the bread until crispy. Break into chunks and put in a food processor. Whiz for a minute or so. If the breadcrumbs seem a little damp, then put them on a baking sheet and toast in a medium oven (180°C/350°F/Gas 4) for a further 5 minutes. Keep an eye on them as they can burn.

GLUTEN-FREE BREADCRUMBS ARE CLOSEST IN TEXTURE TO STORE BOUGHT FISH FINGERS BUT MAY TAKE A LITTLE LONGER TO PREPARE.

CORNFLAKES GIVE A VERY CRUNCHY TOPPING WITH A DISTINCTIVE FLAVOUR THAT MY CHILDREN SEEM TO PREFER.

POLENTA IS VERY QUICK AND EASY AND GIVES A DELICATE CRUNCH.

Macaroni and Cheese SERVES 4–6

This is a very simple and gentle macaroni and cheese. Serve with a fresh green salad or steamed vegetables.

600 ml (1 pint) whole milk
3 garlic cloves
1 bay leaf
375 g (12 oz) uncooked, dried gluten-free pasta
1 tbsp butter
1 tbsp gluten-free plain flour

150 g (5 oz) mature Cheddar or Gruyère cheese, grated
1 tsp gluten-free Dijon mustard
50 ml (2 fl oz) crème fraîche
Parmesan cheese, grated
Salt and pepper

● Pre-heat the oven to 180°C (350°F) Gas 4. Grease an ovenproof dish measuring approximately 20 x 30 cm (8 x 12 in).

● Combine the milk and 3.4 litres of water in a large saucepan. Bring to the boil and add the whole garlic cloves and the bay leaf. Leave to infuse for a few minutes and then remove the garlic and bay leaf along with 150 ml (¼ pint) of the milk and water. Reserve this to make the cheese sauce.

● Bring the large saucepan of milk and water to the boil again and add the pasta. Cook until the pasta is al dente, about 10–12 minutes.

● While the pasta is cooking, make the cheese sauce. In a small saucepan, heat the butter until foamy. Add the flour and stir through but do not allow to brown. Add a little of the reserved milk and water, stirring continuously to make a smooth paste. Continue to add more of the milk and water mixture until you have a sauce-like consistency. Keep the sauce over a low heat, stirring continuously until it comes to the boil It should thicken up slightly and be the consistency of thick cream. Take the sauce off the heat and add the grated cheese, stirring through to melt. Now add the Dijon mustard. Taste and season with salt and pepper as required. Add the crème fraîche and set aside.

● When the pasta is cooked, drain and immediately run through very cold water, to stop the cooking process. Mix the pasta with the cheese sauce and pour into the prepared oven dish. If the mixture looks a little too dry, add a bit more of the reserved milk and water. Dot with butter and scatter the top with grated Parmesan cheese. Bake for 15–20 minutes until piping hot.

COMFORT FOOD YUM!

Polenta Chips (MAKES ABOUT 30 CHIPS)

If I had to choose my favourite recipe from this book it would definitely be this one. Kids love these and adults go completely nuts over them, too! They are fantastic for parties and they are delicious as an accompaniment to meat or fish instead of potatoes or rice.

1 tsp salt
185 g (6½ oz) quick cook polenta
50 g (2 oz) unsalted butter

75 g (3 oz) Parmesan cheese, grated

● In a medium saucepan (a heavy enamelled pan is best) bring 700 ml (1¼ pints) water to the boil. Add the salt, then the polenta in a steady stream stirring with a wooden spoon to prevent lumps. Turn the heat down to a slow simmer while you continue to stir. The polenta will start to thicken in less then a minute. At this time, you will see the bottom of the pan when you draw the spoon across the pan. Turn off the heat.
● Now add the butter. Stir until the butter has been incorporated. Now stir in the cheese. Pour the mixture into a baking dish or a shallow pan. Spread it out evenly to a depth of about 2 cm (¾ in). You do not need to be precise about this, but it's best if it's not too thick or the chips will take longer to cook. Leave the polenta to cool until set, about 30 minutes. Once cool, cover and put in the fridge until you are ready to make the chips.
● Pre-heat the oven to 220°C (425°F) Gas 7.
● Cut the polenta into strips. Aim for something chip-shaped,

approximately 8 cm (3 in) long and 1.5 cm (½ in) wide, or cut into chunky diamonds. Place the chips on an ungreased baking sheet. Bake for 15–20 minutes in a very hot oven.

● The chips are ready when they come off the baking sheet easily. If they are sticking to the baking sheet, put them back in the oven for a few minutes until they release easily. The chips should be lightly golden and crispy on the outside with a lovely soft centre.

 THE CHIPS ARE BEST SERVED STRAIGHT OUT OF THE OVEN. THE POLENTA CAN BE MADE IN ADVANCE AND KEEPS FOR UP TO THREE DAYS IN THE FRIDGE.

JUST CUT AND BAKE THE CHIPS AS AND WHEN YOU NEED THEM.

GREAT FOR PARTIES, PICNICS AND SNACKS

Quick Pizza

(MAKES ABOUT 15–20 PIZZA BASES, 7.5 CM (3 IN) IN DIAMETER)

All my attempts at a 'true' pizza had ended in soggy tasteless bases, until a friend mentioned that she made her children pizza using a scone or biscuit base. I ran all the way home to test out this recipe. Another friend's teenage boys tested the results – they gave it top marks.

275 g (9 oz) gluten-free plain flour
1 tbsp gluten-free baking powder
½ tsp salt
½ tsp xanthan gum
100 g (4 oz) mature Cheddar cheese, grated
250 ml (8 fl oz) crème fraîche
140 ml (5 fl oz) milk

TOPPINGS
Mozzarella
Cheddar cheese
Tomato sauce
Peppers
Mushrooms
Pepperoni
Artichokes
Jalapeños
Roasted vegetables
Olives

● Pre-heat the oven to 200°C (400°F) Gas 6.
● Measure out the flour, baking powder, salt and xanthan gum in a large bowl. Add the grated cheese and mix together. In a separate bowl, combine the crème fraîche and the milk, then pour into the flour mixture and combine with a fork until you get a sticky dough. Turn out onto a floured board.

● Gently knead the dough using a little more flour until it holds together and then roll it out to about 1.5 cm (1/2 in) thickness. Using a 7.5 cm (3 in) floured round cutter, cut out rounds and place these on a baking sheet. Bake in the hot oven for about 10 minutes until the pastry is crisp and golden. In the meantime, prepare your toppings.

● If you are making your pizzas straight away, then once the bases are out of the oven, add your toppings and then put them straight back in the oven for another 10–15 minutes until golden and bubbly. Serve immediately.

● If you are putting the bases in the freezer than leave the bases to cool completely, before you pack them in an airtight container or plastic bags. You do not need to wait for these to defrost before cooking. Simply add your toppings and put in a hot oven. Your baking time may be a little longer.

Note: You may also prefer to make one large pizza. You can easily do this but you will need to adjust your baking time accordingly.

YOU CAN MAKE THE BASES AND FREEZE THEM. TAKE THEM OUT OF THE FREEZER AS NEEDED, PUT ON YOUR PREFERRED TOPPINGS AND BAKE IN THE OVEN FOR 15 MINUTES.

Chocolate Chip Cookies (MAKES ABOUT 50 COOKIES)

A classic cookie, which is as good if not better than any 'normal' cookie and a million miles from the store-bought, gluten-free versions. Serve with ice cold milk.

150 g (5 oz) pecans
200 g (7 oz) gluten-free plain flour
100 g (4 oz) ground almonds
½ tsp bicarbonate of soda
1 tsp gluten-free baking powder
¼ tsp salt

150 g (5 oz) unsalted butter
125 g (4½ oz) caster sugar
125 g (4½ oz) light brown sugar
1 egg
1 tsp vanilla extract
200 g (7 oz) chocolate chips

● Pre-heat the oven to 190°C (375°F) Gas 5.
● Place the pecans on a baking sheet. Toast in the oven for about 10 minutes. Remove from the oven, cool slightly and roughly chop. Set aside.
● Combine the flour, ground almonds, bicarbonate of soda, baking powder and salt in a large bowl. Set aside.
● In a large bowl beat the butter until softened. Add the sugars and beat until light. Add the egg and vanilla extract, then add the flour mixture, followed by the chocolate chips and toasted pecans. Combine well.
● Drop rounded spoonfuls of the dough onto a lined or greased

baking sheet, allowing room for spreading. Bake for 12–15 minutes until golden. Leave to cool for a few minutes before placing on a wire rack. Cool completely before packing into an airtight tin or container.

Note: For young children under 3 replace pecans with raisins, sultanas or chopped, dried apricots.

Cookies

Shrimpy's Chocolate Cake (MAKES 1 LARGE CAKE)

This cake is beautifully moist. The original recipe comes from my grandmother, who we called 'Shrimpy'. I've adapted the recipe from my first cookbook and I think Shrimpy would be very pleased to see that her legendary chocolate cake is now gluten-free!

225 ml (7½ fl oz) milk
1 tbsp white wine vinegar
40 g (1½ oz) cocoa powder
75 ml (3 fl oz) hot water
100 g (4 oz) gluten-free plain flour
85 g (3½ oz) buckwheat flour or ground almonds (see note)
1 tsp bicarbonate of soda

1 tsp gluten-free baking powder
1 tsp xanthan gum
½ tsp salt
100 g (4 oz) unsalted butter
300 g (10 oz) caster sugar
2 eggs
1 tsp vanilla extract
100 g (4 oz) ground almonds

● Pre-heat the oven to 180°C (350°F) Gas 4. Lightly grease and flour a 23 cm (9 in) round, 5 cm (2 in) deep cake tin.

● Combine the milk and vinegar in a bowl and allow to stand for 10 minutes. In another bowl, sift the cocoa powder removing any lumps. Add the hot water, stirring to make a smooth paste and set aside.

● In a large bowl sift the flour, buckwheat flour, bicarbonate of soda, baking powder, xanthan gum and salt and set aside.

● Cream the butter and sugar with an electric mixer until light and

YOU CAN ALSO USE THIS MIXTURE TO MAKE CUPCAKES. IT MAKES ABOUT 24 STANDARD SIZED CUPCAKES.

fluffy. Add the eggs one by one, beating after each addition. Add the vanilla extract. Using a large metal spoon, fold in the ground almonds and the cocoa paste. Now add the flour mixture alternately with the milk mixture, folding through gently. Do not overmix.

● Pour the batter into the prepared tin and bake for 30–40 minutes or until a wooden skewer inserted into the centre comes out clean. Leave to cool for 5 minutes before turning out onto a wire rack. Allow to cool completely before icing with Buttercream Icing (page 199).

Note: Buckwheat flour gives an extra dimension to this cake, making the chocolate flavour stand out a bit more. If you prefer a more neutral flavour, you can substitute additional ground almonds for the buckwheat.

BEAUTIFULLY MOIST! ☆

Ice Cream Sundaes 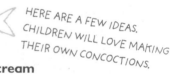 *SERVES 1–2*

Most children love ice cream. This means a gluten-free pudding is always on hand and what better way to make it special than to make ice cream sundaes? Make your own sauces or use commercial ones (check the labels!), if you're short on time.

HERE ARE A FEW IDEAS. CHILDREN WILL LOVE MAKING THEIR OWN CONCOCTIONS.

Peppermint Crunchie Sundae

1 Crunchie bar (check gf)   **Vanilla ice cream**
1 peppermint stick (check gf)   **Chocolate Sauce (page 188)**

● Put the Crunchie bar and peppermint stick in a plastic bag. Smash into pieces with a rolling pin, leaving some largish chunks.
● Put the ice cream in a bowl or in a tall sundae glass. Drizzle with chocolate sauce and top with Crunchie golden peppermint dust.

Sorbet Sundae

Raspberry, mango, passion fruit   **Vanilla ice cream**
sorbet   **Summer Fruit Sauce (page 190)**

● Combine small scoops of each sorbet, layered with a little vanilla ice cream in between. Drizzle fruit sauce on top.

Classic Banana Split

**Vanilla, chocolate, strawberry
ice cream
1 banana, cut into chunks
Chocolate Sauce (page 188)**

**Toffee Sauce (page 189)
Whipped cream
Natural glacé cherries**

● Combine small scoops of each ice cream flavour into a bowl. Add a few chunks of banana. Drizzle with a little chocolate sauce and a little toffee sauce. Top with whipped cream and add a few decorative cherries on top.

LOOK FOR A PREMIUM ICE CREAM MADE WITH CREAM, MILK AND SUGAR. CHECK CAREFULLY AS SOME ICE CREAMS CONTAIN GLUTEN.

Brownie Sundae

**Vanilla and chocolate ice cream
Brownies, cut into smallish chunks
(page 180)
Toffee, Chocolate or Summer Fruit
sauce (see pages 188–90)
Whipped cream (optional)**

● In tall glasses place alternate layers of brownie, vanilla ice cream and chocolate ice cream. Drizzle sauce over the top and add a little spritz of whipped cream.

ICE cream

MY FIVE-YEAR-OLD DAUGHTER CAME UP WITH THE PEPPERMINT CRUNCHIE IDEA, WHICH I WAS RELUCTANT TO TRY AT FIRST BUT I HAVE TO SAY I REALLY LOVE IT!

MUFFINS

breakfast

Breakfast is the most important meal of the day and
can be the trickiest for parents with gluten intolerant
children. I hope some of the recipes in this chapter will
inspire you and give you lots of options to choose from.
Some of these recipes are quick and suitable for everyday
while others may require a little more time and effort and
may be just the thing for a less time-sensitive weekend
breakfast. In many of these recipes you have the option
of making a batch for the freezer. That way a yummy
apple cinnamon muffin or a chocolate chip scone can
be on the cards any day of the week.

Snowy Eggs

SERVES 2

These are a great way to start the day, and are equally delicious for lunch or tea. Both my children were reluctant to eat eggs until I seduced them with these. Part of the attraction is down to the name and, of course, the addition of lovely grated cheese on top helps, too.

4 free-range eggs
Olive oil (optional)

Maldon sea salt (optional)
Parmesan cheese, finely grated

● Fill a medium saucepan with cold water and bring to the boil. Gently lower in the eggs one at a time. Boil for approximately 10 minutes, until the yolks are just set.
● Remove the eggs with a slotted spoon and place under cold running water for at least a minute to prevent them cooking further.
● Peel the eggs and slice them in half. Arrange on a plate and sprinkle with Maldon sea salt, then drizzle with olive oil. Finally, add some grated Parmesan cheese on top.

THESE EGGS MAKE GREAT FINGER FOOD FOR YOUNG BABIES WHEN CUT INTO QUARTERS.

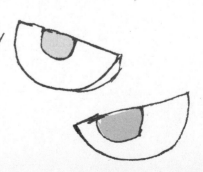

EGGS

VERY TASTY! ☆

Cheese Omelette SERVES 1

This is quick, nutritious and very tasty. Serve for breakfast, lunch or even with chips for a simple supper.

2 eggs	**Parmesan cheese, freshly grated**
Knob of butter	**(or similar)**
2 tbsp milk	**Salt and pepper**

● Break the eggs into a bowl and gently whisk with a fork. Melt the butter in a small skillet or frying pan, until just bubbling.
● Pour the eggs into the skillet and with a small spatula move the eggs from the outside of the pan into the middle. Do this a few times until you have a small mound of softly scrambled eggs.
● Continue to cook for a few more seconds until just starting to set and then sprinkle the grated Parmesan on top. With the spatula, fold the omelette in half and cook for a few more seconds until just crispy.
● Place on a plate, sprinkle with salt and pepper and more cheese. Serve immediately.

Variation: Add strips of ham or cooked vegetables along with the grated cheese.

BREAKFAST

Baked Eggs and Cream

This is a really easy and delicious way to serve eggs that will appeal to the whole family. The eggs are best eaten with something to dip into them: try gluten-free bread or crackers.

Eggs
Butter

Double cream
Salt and pepper

- Pre-heat the oven to 180°C (350°F) Gas 4.
- Allow two eggs per person. Generously grease the required number of ovenproof ramekins with butter.
- Crack your eggs into the ramekins and pour a little double cream on top.
- Prepare a large roasting tin big enough to hold the ramekins. Pour in boiling water and gently place the ramekins in the water. The water should come two thirds of the way up the sides of the ramekins. Place the roasting tin in the preheated oven and bake for 10–12 minutes. Season before serving.

Note: If serving this to a child under 1, you must ensure the yolk is fully set.

REALLY EASY!

Tortilla Espanola *SERVES 4—6*

A true Spanish tortilla, delicious served warm or cold.

Olive oil
2 medium potatoes, peeled and thinly sliced
1 medium onion, finely sliced

1 green (or red) pepper cored, seeded and thinly sliced
1 garlic clove, finely minced
6 large eggs
Salt and pepper

● In a medium sized frying pan pour in enough oil to cover the base of the pan to a depth of 5mm (¼ in). Fry the potatoes in the oil until they are just soft.

● Add the onion to the potatoes and turn the heat down cooking until soft. Next add the pepper and garlic and sprinkle with salt and pepper.

● Beat the eggs in a large bowl. Add the potato, onion and pepper mixture and combine gently with a fork.

● Wipe out the frying pan with kitchen paper and add enough oil to just cover the base of the pan. When the oil is hot add the egg mixture and immediately turn the heat down. Cook over a low heat until just set.

● Flip the tortilla onto a clean plate, wipe out the pan again and add a little more oil. Slide the tortilla back into the pan to cook the other side. Cook on a very low heat for a further 5 minutes until set. Gently loosen from the pan and then turn out onto a plate. Cut into wedges and serve.

BREAKFAST

Granola (MAKES ENOUGH FOR 8–10 SERVINGS)

YOU CAN USE ANY MIXTURE OF NUTS OR SEEDS...

A great breakfast cereal full of wholesome ingredients. It also makes a lovely crunchy topping for yoghurt.

100 g (4 oz) almonds (whole with skin on)
100 g (4 oz) hazelnuts
150 g (5 oz) gluten-free puffed rice

100 g (4 oz) desiccated coconut
50 g (2 oz) raisins
60 ml (2½ fl oz) sunflower oil
100 ml (3½ fl oz) clear honey
40 g (1½ oz) light brown sugar

● Pre-heat the oven to 150°C (300°F) Gas 2.
● In a large bowl combine the almonds, hazelnuts, puffed rice and 75 g (3 oz) of coconut.
● In a small saucepan combine the oil, honey and brown sugar. Heat slowly on a medium to low heat until the sugar has dissolved, but do not allow the mixture to boil.
● Pour the oil mixture over the dry ingredients and stir with a large spoon to ensure the mixture is evenly coated. Place the granola on two large baking sheets making sure it is evenly spread out. Bake for 7–10 minutes and then stir through. Bake for a further 7–10 minutes until the mixture is very lightly browned.
● Remove from the baking sheets and place back in the large bowl. Add the raisins and the remaining coconut and stir through. Allow to cool thoroughly before placing in an airtight jar or tin. The mixture will keep for about 1 month.

Note: This recipe is unsuitable for children below the age of 3.

Three Bears Porridge with Maple Syrup SERVES 1

This warming little porridge will keep winter at bay. Brown rice flakes are a nutritious alternative to oats. The texture is very soft but not mushy so this is an ideal breakfast food for young babies and toddlers.

25 g (1 oz) brown rice flakes
150 ml (¼ pint) whole milk
Butter

Maple syrup (optional)
Salt (optional)

● Measure out the rice flakes into a small bowl. Add some cold water to cover completely and leave to soak for about 5 minutes.
● Drain the rice flakes and discard the water. Add the rice flakes to a small pan and then pour in the milk. Stir over a gentle heat until just simmering. Add butter to taste and serve immediately, either with maple syrup or sprinkle a little bit of Maldon sea salt on top for a savoury version.

BREAKFAST

Date and Apple Breakfast Bars

(MAKES ABOUT 24 BARS)

These very yummy bars, packed with minerals and vitamins, make a wholesome breakfast treat or mid-morning snack. Delicious warm out of the oven, they will keep for a few days in the fridge. They are also really good for picnics!

Sunflower oil, for greasing
150 g (5 oz) chopped dates
75 g (3 oz) whole almonds
50 g (2 oz) sesame seeds
1 large apple, about 150 g (5 oz)
40 g (1½ oz) gluten-free plain flour
25 g (1 oz) ground almonds

1 tsp ground cinnamon
1 tsp gluten-free baking powder
½ tsp salt
50 g (2 oz) butter, melted
85 g (3½ oz) light brown sugar
2 eggs
1 tsp vanilla extract

● Pre-heat the oven 170°C (325°F) Gas 3.
● Line a 23-cm (9-in) square pan with aluminium foil. Dip a pastry brush in sunflower oil and lightly grease the pan, making sure you get into the corners.
● If the dates are not soft, soak them in boiling water for a few minutes to rehydrate them. Then, drain the water and roughly chop. Toast the almonds in the oven for about 10 minutes until golden and leave to cool. Roughly chop and set aside. Place the sesame seeds in a small skillet or frying pan and toast until lightly

GREAT ♡ ♡
FOR SNACKS,

golden. Set aside. Peel and core the apple and chop into bite-sized chunks.

● In a medium bowl combine the flour, ground almonds, cinnamon, baking powder and salt. Add the dates, toasted almonds, sesame seeds and apple and mix together.

● In a separate bowl combine the melted butter, brown sugar, eggs and vanilla. Add this to the date and flour mixture and combine well. Spread the mixture into the prepared pan and bake for 20–25 minutes until golden.

● Leave to stand for 5 minutes before turning out onto a wire rack. Gently peel the tin foil from the base. Leave to cool before slicing into bars.

Variation: To make fig and pear bars, replace the dates with dried figs and the apple with pear.

Note: If you are making these for very young children below the age of 3, please omit the whole almonds.

PICNICS AND
LUNCH BOXES

BREAKFAST

Maurice's Dried Fruit Compote SERVES 4

Maurice Sirkin, a good friend and fantastic cook, used to make this delicious compote. The addition of ginger and vanilla gives you a lovely warm glow inside.

65 g (2½ oz) caster sugar
1 vanilla pod
4 strips of lemon rind
1 cinnamon stick
1 small piece of fresh root ginger, smashed

300 g (10 oz) dried fruit, such as prunes, apricots, pears and plums
Natural yoghurt, to serve

● In a saucepan combine the sugar, vanilla, lemon rind, cinnamon and ginger with 100 ml (3½ fl oz) of water. Bring to the boil and then simmer until the sugar has dissolved.
● Add the dried fruit, stir, cover and simmer on a very low heat for 10 minutes until the fruit is soft (but not mushy). Add more water if necessary. Leave to cool then serve on its own or with natural yoghurt.

Big Ruthie's Apple Compote SERVES 6

This is a very delicious apple compote, which you can serve with yoghurt or as a classic accompaniment to potato latkes. We love it cold, straight out of the fridge drizzled with a little double cream, but it's really yummy just plain too.

6–8 green apples (such as Granny Smith), peeled, cored and cut into quarters
100 g (4 oz) light brown or caster sugar

1 tsp ground cinnamon
A pinch of ground nutmeg
Freshly squeezed juice of ½ lemon

● Place the prepared apples in a medium saucepan. Add 150 ml (¼ pint) water and cook over medium heat for 15–20 minutes until the apples are soft. You may need to add a bit more water, so keep an eye on them while they are cooking. Add only enough water to keep the mixture soft and moist and prevent it burning.

● When the apples are soft, remove from the heat and add the sugar, mashing down the apples, to make a chunky purée. Add the cinnamon, nutmeg and lemon juice. Taste and add more sugar or lemon juice if required. Place in a bowl and refrigerate until needed. Serve the apple compote warm or cold.

Seasonal Fruit Plate

This works really well in our household. A beautifully presented plate of fresh seasonal fruit for breakfast will make sure they get a good dose of vitamin C first thing in the morning. You can also add a fruity yoghurty dip, which will really appeal to young children. Select two or three fruits of contrasting colours and textures. Here are a few suggestions:

Mango, peeled and sliced into chunks
Melon, peeled and sliced
Oranges
Clementines
Bananas
Cherries
Strawberries
Raspberries

Blueberries
Nectarines
Peaches
Pears
Kiwi fruit
Pineapple chunks
Apples
Grapes

To make dip

Squirt a little clear honey or a spoonful of Summer Fruit Sauce (page 190) into some Greek yoghurt. Stir to combine.

GOOD FOR ♡ ♡
A SNACK

USE WHATEVER YOU'VE
GOT IN THE FRUIT BOWL,
BUT MAKE SURE IT'S IN
SEASON, FRESH AND RIPE.

Banana

FRESH
AND RIPE

BREAKFAST

Smoothies SERVES 1

These are a good way to get fruit into your children's diet.
There are no hard-and-fast rules but I've found the best way
to get a really luxurious texture akin to a thick milkshake, is
to use frozen bananas and juice instead of milk.

You can freeze bananas when they are at their best. Peel and
cut them into halves or thirds. Put them into plastic bags or
containers and keep them in the freezer until needed. They
will keep for about 1 month. I use a hand-held blender to make
smoothies, but a normal blender or liquidiser will work too.

Here are a few combinations to get you started. You can
use fresh or frozen berries if you prefer. It's also handy
to have a sieve, as some fruits, like
blueberries and raspberries, have little
seeds, which some children will find
off-putting. I often use tubes of flavoured
yoghurt, but you can use natural yoghurt
sweetened with a little honey, if you prefer.

Smoothie

Cherry Smoothie

½ frozen banana
Apple juice
5–6 cherries, pitted

1 strawberry yoghurt
tube, or 2 tbsp natural
yoghurt

FRUITY!

Mango Nectarine Smoothie

½ frozen banana
Orange juice
½ mango, peeled and chopped

½ nectarine, peeled and chopped
1 apricot yoghurt tube or
2 tbsp natural yoghurt

Raspberry Smoothie

1 small handful of frozen
raspberries
Apple juice

½ nectarine, peeled and chopped
1 raspberry yoghurt tube or
2 tbsp natural yoghurt

Banana chocolate smoothie

½ frozen banana
Milk
2 tsp cocoa powder, dissolved in
a little hot water

A good scoop of vanilla or
chocolate ice cream (optional)

To make smoothie

● Place the fruit (frozen banana or raspberries, etc) in a tall container (preferably the jug which comes with your hand-held blender).
● Add enough juice or milk to cover it and leave to sit for a few minutes.
● Now add the rest of the ingredients and whiz until completely smooth. If it's too thick, add a little more juice to thin down to the right consistency.
● Pour into a tall glass and enjoy!

Buttermilk Pancakes *SERVES 4*

These crisp, light and tangy pancakes are great served with maple syrup, jam or honey. For a savoury version, serve with strips of crispy bacon.

50 g (2 oz) gluten-free plain flour
45 g (1½ oz) ground almonds
1½ tsp gluten-free baking powder
1 tsp sugar
½ tsp salt
200 ml (7 fl oz) buttermilk

1 egg
Milk
2 tbsp butter
Sunflower oil
Maple syrup, to serve

● In a medium bowl combine the flour, almonds, baking powder, sugar and salt. Mix gently with a fork. Add the buttermilk, egg and a little milk to make a thickish batter (the consistency of double cream). Mix and leave to sit for a few minutes.

● Melt the butter in a small skillet or frying pan and add to the batter. Add a little more butter and sunflower oil to the same skillet and heat until hot. Add a dollop of pancake batter and swirl in the pan. Cook the pancake on one side until bubbles appear and then flip on to the other side. Cook for a few seconds more. Serve immediately with butter and maple syrup.

Note: You can substitute 200 ml milk mixed with 1 ½ tsp white vinegar for buttermilk.

THE MOST IMPORTANT THING WHEN MAKING PANCAKES IS THE HEAT OF THE PAN. TOO HOT AND THE PANCAKES WILL SCORCH, TOO COLD AND THEY WILL BE A BIT LIMP.

WHEN YOU ADD THE BATTER TO THE PAN IT SHOULD SIZZLE.

COOKED TREATS

Potato Latkes SERVES 2–3

A real breakfast treat, but you can serve them anytime. Have everyone seated and waiting for the full wow effect as you serve them straight off the griddle. This makes a small batch so you may want to up the quantities once you've tried them.

**2 medium potatoes, about 300 g
(10 oz), peeled
½ egg, beaten**

**Sunflower oil
Salt**

● Coarsely grate the potatoes, then rinse them in cold running water for a few minutes and drain. Put the potatoes in a clean tea towel and squeeze out as much liquid as you can. This is an important step to ensure you get light crispy pancakes.
● Place the potato in a medium bowl. Add the egg and season with salt and pepper, mixing together well.
● Add enough sunflower oil to cover the base of a small skillet or frying pan to a depth of about 1 cm (⅜ in). Heat the oil until hot but not smoking. Add one or two dollops of potato mixture to the pan and fry gently until golden on one side. Turn and cook on the other side until golden. Place on a piece of kitchen paper to drain off excess oil and sprinkle with a little sea salt. Serve immediately, or keep warm in a a low oven while you cook the remainder of the mixture.

Corn Fritters (MAKES ABOUT 6 FRITTERS)

Quick to make, these fritters make a wholesome filling breakfast. The recipe was inspired by Arepas de Chocolo, which are amazing little corn cakes that you can buy on the roadside in Colombia.

2 fresh corn cobs (see note)
50 g (2 oz) mature Cheddar cheese, grated
1 egg
4 tbsp milk

2 tbsp polenta
Butter
Sunflower oil
Salt and pepper

● With a sharp knife, cut the niblets of corn off the cobs. Put all of the ingredients, excluding the oil, in a bowl and blitz with a hand-held blender or whiz in a food processor until mushy. The mixture will be thick but should still pour.

● Heat a skillet or griddle pan until quite hot. Add a little butter and some sunflower oil and when hot add a few tablespoons of the fritter batter. Cook until just set and golden. Flip and cook the other side for a few seconds. Serve immediately.

Note: You can substitute 100 g (4 oz) frozen or canned sweetcorn.

VERY TASTY!

Classic French Toast SERVES 2–3

To my great delight, gluten-free bread works really well in this. When I first tried out this recipe, my children were enthralled by the idea of being allowed icing sugar for breakfast – they literally licked their plates clean!

I egg, lightly beaten
Milk
A few drops of vanilla extract
4 slices gluten-free bread

Butter
Sunflower oil
Icing sugar

● In a medium bowl combine the egg, a splash of milk and vanilla extract. Dip a slice of bread in the eggy mixture – make sure both sides are well coated, but do not allow the bread to become soggy as it will fall apart in the pan.
● Heat a mixture of butter and oil in a small skillet or frying pan. Heat until hot, but not smoking. Put the eggy bread in the skillet and cook for a minute or so on each side until golden and crispy. Transfer to a plate and sprinkle with icing sugar and serve. Repeat the process with the remaining bread.

BREAKFAST

Blueberry Muffins

(MAKES 6–8 LARGE MUFFINS, 12–16 STANDARD MUFFINS OR 24–36 MINI MUFFINS)

With a hint of nutmeg and lots of juicy blueberries, serve these muffins with lots of fresh butter. Best eaten freshly baked out of the oven, but if you find you have some left over, they also freeze very well.

150 ml (¼ pint) milk
1 tbsp white wine vinegar
150 g (5 oz) gluten-free plain flour
150 g (5 oz) ground almonds
2¼ tsp gluten-free baking powder
1 tsp xanthan gum
¼ tsp grated nutmeg
¼ tsp ground cinnamon
½ tsp salt
150 g (5 oz) unsalted butter
125 g (4½ oz) caster sugar
3 eggs
150 g (5 oz) fresh blueberries (or frozen)

● Pre-heat the oven to 180°C (350°F) Gas 4. Lightly grease a 6–hole extra large muffin tin, a 12-hole standard muffin tin or two 12-hole mini muffin tins.

● In a small bowl combine the milk and vinegar and allow to stand for a few minutes. In a medium bowl combine the flour, ground almonds, baking powder, xanthan gum, nutmeg, cinnamon and salt.

● Using an electric beater, whisk the butter until pale and then add the sugar gradually until the mixture is light and fluffy. Add the eggs one at a time, beating well after each addition. The mixture should look like mayonnaise. Now add the flour mixture alternately with the milk and vinegar mixture, folding gently to

GORGEOUS FRESH! ♡ ♡

mix together. Fold in the blueberries.

● Working quickly, divide the mixture into the prepared tin. Bake for 25–30 minutes for large muffins, 10–15 minutes for standard or 8–10 minutes for mini muffins. To test if they are cooked through, insert a wooden skewer into the centre. If it comes out clean the muffins are cooked. Allow to cool in the tin for a few minutes before serving.

Variations: You can use the Streusel Topping recipe (page 96) to make streusel muffins and you can also substitute other fruit for the blueberries, such as raspberries or bananas.

Instructions for freezing: Pack in an airtight container and divide with layers of greaseproof paper. Leave to defrost before eating.

MUFFINS

Cinnamon Apple Streusel Muffins

(MAKES 6–8 LARGE MUFFINS, 12–16 STANDARD MUFFINS OR 24–36 MINI MUFFINS)

The smell of apples and cinnamon when these muffins are baking is very inviting. The addition of a crispy, sugary topping simply adds to the luxury.

150 g (5 oz) soured cream
150 g (5 oz) ground almonds
150 g (5 oz) gluten-free flour
2¼ tsp gluten-free baking powder
½ tsp ground nutmeg
1 tsp ground cinnamon
1 tsp xanthan gum
½ tsp salt
150 g (5 oz) unsalted butter
125 g (4½ oz) caster sugar
3 eggs
150 g (5 oz) apple, peeled, cored and chopped

FOR THE STREUSEL TOPPING
65 g (2½ oz) soft light brown sugar
2 tbsp gluten-free plain flour
25 g (1 oz) cold, unsalted butter
50 g (2 oz) chopped nuts (hazelnuts, almonds, pecans)

● Pre-heat the oven to 180°C (350°F) Gas 4. Lightly grease a 6–hole large muffin tin, a 12-hole standard muffin tin or 24-hole mini muffin tin.

● Make the streusel topping. Combine the sugar and flour. Cut the butter into small chunks and add to the sugar-flour mixture. Using your fingers, gently rub together to incorporate the butter.

GOOD ♡ ♡
FOR FREEZING

Add the chopped nuts and mix together. Set aside.

● In a medium bowl combine the flour, ground almonds, baking powder, xanthan gum, nutmeg, cinnamon and salt.

● Using an electric beater, whisk the butter until pale and then add the sugar gradually until the mixture is light and fluffy. Add the eggs one at a time, beating well after each addition. The mixture should look like mayonnaise. Now add the flour mixture alternately with the soured cream, folding gently to mix together. Fold in the chopped apples.

● Working quickly, divide the mixture into the prepared tins. Place a spoonful of topping on each muffin. Bake for 25–30 minutes for large muffins, 10–15 minutes for standard muffins or 8–10 minutes for mini muffins. To test if they are cooked through, insert a wooden skewer into the centre. If it comes out clean the muffins are cooked. Allow to cool in the tin for a few minutes before serving.

Note: Omit streusel topping if serving to children under 3.

THESE FREEZE WELL, SO YOU CAN MAKE A BATCH AND SQUIRREL SOME AWAY FOR A RAINY DAY.

BREAKFAST

Cornbread (MAKES 1 LOAF)

An American favourite, this can be used for breakfast served with butter and jam, to make sandwiches or even as a delicious stuffing. I like to keep a few pieces wrapped in foil in the freezer – put the parcel straight into a hot oven and you will have warm toasted cornbread ready for breakfast in about 15 minutes.

75 g (3 oz) unsalted butter
65 g (2½ oz) gluten-free plain or buckwheat flour
225 g (7½ oz) quick cook polenta or corn meal
1 tsp salt
1 tsp caster sugar
1 tbsp gluten-free baking powder
2 eggs, well beaten
275 ml (9 fl oz) milk
50 ml (2 fl oz) natural yoghurt

● Pre-heat the oven to 240°C (475°F) Gas 9, or the hottest setting.
● Melt the butter and leave to cool. Dip a pastry brush in the melted butter and lightly grease a 22 cm (8½ in) square tin.
● Combine the flour, polenta, salt, sugar and baking powder in a large bowl. Make a well in the centre and add the eggs, milk and yoghurt. Stir to combine with a fork. Add the remaining melted butter and mix gently until just combined.
● Pour the mixture into the prepared tin. Bake for 15 minutes or until a wooden skewer inserted in the centre comes out clean. Leave to cool in the tin for a few minutes then cut into squares and serve.

DELICIOUS WARM! ♡ ♡

Note: The type or brand of polenta used can give you very different batters. If the batter seems very thick and reluctant to pour out of the bowl, add a little more milk. If the batter seems very liquidy, add a little more polenta. The ideal consistency should be like a thick cake batter.

Cornbread
↓

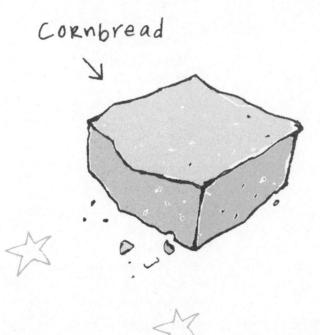

BREAKFAST

Chocolate Chip Scones (MAKES 8–12 SCONES)

These yummy scones are light and tasty – just the thing for breakfast, tea time or picnics. They also make a delicious break time treat for school lunch boxes. As they freeze well, keep a few in the freezer in case of last minute emergencies!

275 g (9 oz) gluten-free plain flour
50 g (2 oz) buckwheat flour or ground almonds
3 tsp gluten-free baking powder
2 tsp xanthan gum
1 tsp salt
4 tbsp caster sugar

100 g (4 oz) cold unsalted butter
100 g (4 oz) chocolate chips
2 eggs
125 ml (4 fl oz) natural yoghurt or buttermilk
Demerara sugar
Milk

● Pre-heat the oven to 240°C (475°F) Gas 9, or the hottest setting. Line a baking sheet with baking paper.

● Combine the flour, buckwheat, baking powder, xanthan gum, salt and sugar in a large bowl. Cut the butter into small chunks and add to the dry ingredients. Using your fingertips, rub the butter into the flour until incorporated and it resembles breadcrumbs, then add the chocolate chips.

● Combine the eggs and yoghurt and whisk lightly with a fork. Make a well in the centre of the dry ingredients and then pour in the yoghurt and egg mixture. Using a fork bring the ingredients together to form a dough, adding a little more flour if necessary. Turn the dough onto a lightly floured surface and knead gently into a round disk. Using your hand, tap the disc and flatten to about 3 cm (1¼ in) thick. Using a sharp knife, cut the disc into two halves. Now cut each half into triangular wedges. Transfer these onto the lined baking sheet. Repeat the process with the remaining half.

● Brush the tops of the wedges with a little milk and sprinkle with demerara sugar. Place in a hot oven and bake for approximately 10 minutes until lightly golden. Transfer to a wire rack and leave to cool for a few minutes before serving.

Variations

For cheese scones: Omit the chocolate chips and sugar. Add 100 g (4 oz) grated Gruyère cheese to the flour mixture after you've rubbed in the butter. Continue as per the recipe. Brush the scones with a light egg wash and sprinkle with sesame seeds.

For cherry scones: Substitute 100 g (4 oz) of dried cherries for the chocolate chips. Soak the cherries in a little hot water for 15 minutes. Drain well and then add them to the rubbed in flour mixture. Continue as per the recipe.

...OR PICNICS

BREAKFAST

Banana Bread <small>(MAKES 1 LARGE LOAF OR 24 STANDARD-SIZED MUFFINS)</small>

I adapted this fantastic recipe from my aunt Ruthie's repertoire – it works really well as a gluten-free version. It makes a tasty, nutritious breakfast, especially when you are on the run.

100 g (4 oz) pecan nuts, walnuts or hazelnuts - optional (see note)
100 g (4 oz) unsalted butter
150 g (5 oz) caster sugar
125 g (4½ oz) light brown sugar
2 eggs, beaten
1½ tsp vanilla extract
185 g (6½ oz) gluten-free plain flour
125g (4½ oz) ground almonds
1½ tsp gluten-free baking powder
1 tsp baking soda
1 tsp xanthan gum
1 tsp salt
350 g (11½ oz) mashed bananas (about 3 medium bananas)
175 ml (6 fl oz) buttermilk

FOR THE ICING
Freshly squeezed juice of
½ lemon
5–6 tbsp icing sugar

● Pre-heat the oven to 180°C (350°F) Gas 4. If you are using nuts, toast them lightly for about 10 minutes. Roughly chop and leave to cool.

● Meanwhile, line a 23 x 13 cm (9 x 5 in) loaf tin with a greaseproof paper liner. If you are making muffins then you will require 24 muffin or cupcake liners.

● In a medium bowl cream the butter and sugars until light. Add the eggs a little at a time, beating well after each addition. Add the vanilla extract.

GOOD ♡ ♡
FOR FREEZING

● Combine the flour, ground almonds, baking powder, baking soda, xanthan gum and salt in a medium bowl. Mash the bananas. Add the bananas to the butter and sugar mixture and stir. Add the flour mixture alternately with the buttermilk, mixing well with each addition. Pour the mixture into the prepared tin (or muffin tins). Bake for 45 minutes for a large loaf or 12–15 minutes for muffins. The loaf or muffins are ready when a wooden skewer inserted in the middle comes out clean.

● While the bread is in the oven make the icing. Combine the lemon juice with the icing sugar to make an opaque liquid. It should pour easily off a spoon but not be too liquidy. Adjust to the right consistency by adding more sugar or lemon juice as required.

● When the bread is ready, remove from the oven and allow to cool for about 10 minutes. Drizzle the icing on the bread or muffins and allow to cool. If you are freezing the bread, then do not ice it. Take it out of the freezer and allow it to defrost before icing.

Note: For children under 3 omit the chopped nuts and replace with sultanas or raisins.

THIS RECIPE WILL MAKE ABOUT 100 MINI MUFFINS. BAKE FOR ABOUT 7–10 MINUTES IN THE OVEN.

BREAKFAST

Cheesy Snakes (MAKES APPROXIMATELY 20–25 SNAKES)

This recipe is really easy and one which children enjoy getting involved in. The cheesy snakes make great breakfast food and are also perfect as an after-school snack. They are at their best straight out of the oven, but you can also freeze them.

250 g (8 oz) gluten-free plain flour
1 tbsp gluten-free baking powder
½ tsp salt
1 tsp mustard powder
½ tsp xanthan gum

100 g (4 oz) medium or strong Cheddar cheese, grated
200 ml (7 fl oz) crème fraîche
50 ml (2 fl oz) natural yoghurt
150 ml (¼ pint) milk

● Pre-heat the oven to 220°C (425°F) Gas 7. Line a baking sheet with a greaseproof liner.

● In a large bowl combine the flour, baking powder, salt, mustard and xanthan gum. Add the grated cheese and mix together.

● Combine the crème fraîche, yoghurt and milk in a jug and whisk the mixture with a fork. Make a well in the centre of the flour and cheese mixture and then pour in the liquid. Bring the mixture together with a fork until you have a sticky dough. Resist the temptation to add lots more flour – the dough will be sticky, but you will not need to handle it very much.

● Lightly flour a board or work surface. Turn the dough out on to the surface and very gently tap it into a round disk. With your hands pat the disk down evenly to a thickness of about 1.5 cm

GREAT FOR SNACKS

(½ in). Cut into strips and then cut each strip in half. Using a palette knife, gently place these on a lined baking sheet. Bake for approximately 10 minutes until lightly golden. Transfer to a wire rack and leave to cool for a few minutes.

I USUALLY WRAP A FEW OF THESE IN FOIL AND KEEP THEM STASHED AWAY IN THE FREEZER.

YOU CAN POP THEM STRAIGHT INTO A HOT OVEN, CONVENIENTLY WRAPPED IN THEIR LITTLE FOIL OVERCOATS, AND THEY WILL BE READY TO EAT IN ABOUT 15 MINUTES.

...OR PICNICS

Date Bread *(MAKES 1 LARGE LOAF)*

This loaf, with chewy chunks of dates, can be used to make delicious cream cheese and smoked ham sandwiches. Alternatively, it is also a lovely tea bread. Just spread with some fresh creamy butter and serve with a big mug of tea or hot cocoa.

150 g (5 oz) dates
100 g (4oz) caster sugar
200 g (7 oz) gluten-free plain flour
185 g (6½ oz) ground almonds
½ tsp salt

1 tsp xanthan gum
1 tbsp gluten-free baking powder
275 ml (9 fl oz) milk
1 egg
85 g (3½ oz) butter, melted
2 tbsp grated lemon zest

● Pre-heat the oven 190°C (375°F) Gas 5. Line a 23 x 13 cm (9 x 5 in) loaf tin with a greaseproof liner or grease lightly.
● Soak the dates in a little boiling water to soften for 5–10 minutes. Drain the water from the dates and chop them into even pieces. Set aside.
● Combine the sugar, flour, almonds, salt, xanthan gum and baking powder in a large bowl and make a well in the centre. Add the milk and egg and mix gently, then stir in the melted butter, dates and lemon zest.
● Pour the mixture into the prepared tin. Bake 40–45 minutes or until a skewer inserted into the centre of the loaf comes out clean. Leave to cool in the tin for 5 minutes before turning out on to a wire rack. Allow to cool completely before serving.

GOOD FOR A SNACK

Cocoa

Sandwich

CHUNKS OF DATES

PUMPKIN SOUP

lunch and light snacks

Soups, sandwiches and salads are the order of the day for most people at lunchtime and this can be a problem if you are gluten intolerant. Lunch is the meal we are most likely to have out and the majority of cafeterias, cafés, coffee bars and snack bars simply do not cater for the gluten-free. Well, it's time to get creative. There are lots of things to choose from in this chapter, from quick soups, which are nutritious, filling and portable to a good selection of child-friendly salads, tacos and crêpes. Ideas for picnics and lunch boxes are also included.

Kiddy Corn Chowder *SERVES 4*

Children love sweetcorn and certainly my children can't seem to get enough of it. Here's a quick soup that can be served two ways, either chunky or smooth.

2 tbsp unsalted butter
I small onion, finely chopped
3–4 rashers of pancetta or bacon (optional)
I medium potato, peeled and diced

300 g (10 oz) frozen sweetcorn
400 ml (14 fl oz) gluten-free chicken stock
I bay leaf
200 ml (7 fl oz) whole milk

● In a medium pan melt the butter, then add the onion and cook until soft and translucent (but don't brown it). Add the pancetta or bacon, if using, and cook gently for a few minutes. Add the potato and mix through, followed by the sweetcorn. Add the stock and bay leaf and simmer over medium heat for about 20 minutes until the potato is soft. Add the milk, warm through and serve.

sieve

IF YOU PREFER A SILKY SOUP WITHOUT BITS, THEN BLEND IN BATCHES AND PUT THROUGH A FINE SIEVE.

SNACKS

Quick Vegetable Soup

This is a good soup to have up your sleeve on a rainy day, using any vegetables you have to hand.

I tbsp unsalted butter

2 tbsp olive oil

I medium onion, finely chopped

I leek, rinsed and finely chopped

2 celery sticks, finely chopped

I garlic clove, finely chopped

I tsp dried thyme

2 medium carrots, peeled and diced

2 small potatoes, peeled and diced

I litre (1¾ pints) gluten-free chicken stock

I bay leaf

I large handful of French beans, trimmed and cut into 3 cm (1¼ in) pieces

10 small cherry tomatoes, skinned and diced

Freshly chopped flat leaf parsley or basil (optional)

Salt and pepper

● In a medium saucepan melt the butter and olive oil. Sweat the onion in the oil for a few minutes until wilted and translucent but not brown. Add the leek, celery and garlic and cook for a minute or so, then add the thyme and seasoning.

● Add the carrot and potatoes and cook for a few minutes, then add the chicken stock along with the bay leaf. Cook for 10 minutes until the carrot and potato are soft. Add the French beans and cook for a further 5 minutes.

● Just before serving add the chopped tomato and a scattering of freshly chopped herbs, such as parsley or basil.

LUNCH AND LIGHT

Creamy Tomato Soup SERVES 4

This is a healthy alternative to the canned version. It takes a bit of work to get the right texture, but the results are heavenly and you can rest assured your loved ones are getting a big dose of vitamin C.

500 g (1 lb) cherry tomatoes or ripe tomatoes
2 red peppers
1 red onion, peeled and chopped into large chunks
3 garlic cloves
Olive oil
1 tbsp butter
1 tbsp olive oil

1 onion, finely sliced
1 large carrot, peeled and chopped
1 sprig of fresh rosemary
1 bay leaf
500 ml (17 fl oz) gluten-free chicken stock
Double cream (optional), to serve
Salt and pepper

● Pre-heat the oven to 220°C (425°F) Gas 7.

● Put the tomatoes, peppers, red onion and garlic cloves (unpeeled) in a roasting tin. Drizzle with olive oil and season with salt and pepper. Roast in the oven for 30 minutes. The vegetables should be soft but not burned.

● In a medium-sized pot or saucepan melt the butter and olive oil. Add the finely sliced onion and cook until translucent. Stir in the carrot and add the roasted vegetables, the herbs and the stock. Rinse out the roasting tin with a bit of the stock to get all the lovely jammy flavours from the tin.

● Cover and simmer the soup for about 30 minutes until everything

SNACKS

is soft. Then, using either a hand-held blender or food processor, blend the soup in batches. Put the liquid through a fine sieve and press to get all the delicious juice out. This does take a bit of elbow grease, but I think it's worth it. You will have a gorgeous red and silky tomato soup.

● Reheat gently when you are ready to serve the soup and add, if you like, a splash of double cream just before serving for the finishing touch.

Rice Soup SERVES 4

Simple but very restorative, this is a good soup when the cupboard is a bit bare and you can't face going to the shops.

2 tbsp unsalted butter
1 tbsp olive oil
1 medium onion, finely chopped
2 celery sticks, finely diced
1 garlic clove, minced
2 tbsp uncooked rice (arborio, basmati or long grain)

1 carrot, peeled and diced
1 medium potato, peeled and diced
500 ml (17 fl oz) gluten-free chicken stock
1 bay leaf
Salt and pepper

● Melt the butter and olive oil in a medium pan. Add the onion and sweat until soft and translucent but not brown. Add the celery and garlic and fry for a few more minutes, without browning. Stir in the rice, then add the potato and carrot.

● Add the chicken stock and bay leaf, cover and simmer for about 15 minutes. Season with salt and pepper and serve.

Aunt Ruthie's Amazing Pumpkin Soup *SERVES 8–10*

Here's a real gem from my amazing aunt Ruthie. This makes a lot of soup, but you can either halve the recipe or freeze some for a rainy day.

100 g (4 oz) unsalted butter
2 large onions, coarsely chopped
4 garlic cloves, peeled and chopped
4 celery sticks, washed and sliced
2 kg (4 lb) pumpkin, peeled, deseeded and diced
6–8 medium carrots, peeled and diced
6–8 medium sweet potatoes, peeled and diced

1 bay leaf, broken in half
A few sprigs of fresh thyme
2 litres (3½ pints) gluten-free chicken stock
200 ml (7 fl oz) dry sherry or dry white wine
Freshly chopped flat leaf parsley, to garnish
Salt and pepper

● Melt the butter in a large saucepan. Add the onion and garlic and cook over low heat until translucent but don't allow to brown. Add the celery, pumpkin, carrots, sweet potatoes, bay leaf and thyme.

● Mix together and add about 250 ml (8 fl oz) of stock (or just enough to cover the vegetables) and the sherry. Simmer uncovered for 30 minutes.

● Add the remainder of the stock, cover and simmer for a further 40 minutes. Season with salt and pepper during the last 10

SNACKS

minutes of cooking and remove the bay leaf and sprigs of thyme.
● You can serve the soup as is, or you can blend it in batches for a very luxurious creamy texture, with the consistency of thick double cream. You may want to thin it out a little once blended – add a little more chicken stock or water to thin down until you get the right consistency. Serve garnished with freshly chopped flat leaf parsley.

Note: I like blending about a third of the soup and then adding the silky purée to what's left in the pot. That way you get the best of both worlds.

IF YOU ARE CONCERNED ABOUT THE USE OF SHERRY, IT IS WORTH NOTING THAT IF YOU SIMMER IT FOR A FEW MINUTES ALL OF THE ALCOHOL WILL EVAPORATE ANYWAY.

PUMPKIN SOUP

YOU CAN CHOOSE TO LEAVE IT OUT, BUT IT DOES ADD A LOVELY DIMENSION TO THE SOUP.

Lucia's Bean Soup *SERVES 4*

My youngest daughter loves this soup. I use canned beans, which means you can make a tasty, filling soup in about 15 minutes.

2 tbsp olive oil
1 tbsp unsalted butter
1 medium onion, chopped
2 garlic cloves, minced
2 sticks celery, finely sliced
2 tsp ground coriander
1 tsp ground cumin
480 g (15 oz) red kidney beans, drained

400–600 ml (14 fl oz–1 pint) gluten-free chicken stock
2 tsp liquid chicken stock
1 bay leaf
8 cherry tomatoes (or 2 medium tomatoes), skinned and chopped, plus extra to garnish
1 avocado, peeled, stoned and chopped, to garnish
Salt and pepper

● Melt the butter and olive oil in a medium pan. Add the onion and cook until soft and translucent. Add the garlic, celery, coriander, cumin and season with salt and pepper. Stir well and cook for a few minutes without browning.

● Drain the beans and rinse with cold water. Add the beans to the pan and stir together. Add the chicken stocks, bay leaf, and tomatoes. Cover and simmer for 10–15 minutes. Serve as a chunky soup or blend in batches – remove the bay leaf first! Garnish with fresh tomato and avocado chunks.

I'VE USED RED KIDNEY BEANS, BUT YOU COULD USE ANY CANNED BEANS YOU HAVE IN THE CUPBOARD, SUCH AS CANNELLINI, BORLOTTI OR BUTTER BEANS.

SNACKS

GREAT FOR PICNICS AND LUNCHBOXES

Pasta Salad · SERVES 4

This is a great picnic or lunch box salad, as it seems to get better the longer it stands. But take care not to overcook the pasta – soggy pasta is really unpleasant.

150 g (5 oz) dried, uncooked gluten-free pasta

12 ripe cherry tomatoes, quartered

50 g (2 oz) olives, pitted and chopped

4–5 sun-dried tomatoes, chopped

3 tsp capers

Toasted pine nuts (optional)

Olive oil

Freshly squeezed lemon juice

Maldon sea salt

Freshly grated Parmesan cheese

● Cook the pasta as normal in plenty of boiling water, taking care not to overcook. Drain and rinse in cold water to stop the pasta cooking further.

● Meanwhile, place the chopped tomatoes, olives, sun-dried tomatoes and capers in a medium bowl. Add a good sprinkle of salt and a glug of olive oil. Mix gently to combine and leave to stand a few minutes while you finish cooking the pasta.

● Put the cooked, well drained pasta in the bowl with all the other ingredients. Toss gently to combine. Taste for seasoning, add a little more oil if necessary, a squeeze of lemon juice and salt. Add the pine nuts and combine. Don't overmix as the pasta may start to disintegrate.

● Leave to marinate for at least an hour before serving. You can keep the salad in the fridge overnight, but it's best served at room temperature.

Rice Salad à la Giorgi

SERVES 4

This recipe was inspired by a delicious salad we had in a little village called Giorgi, in Italy, many years ago. Our friend, Marinella, prepared this as a starter made with Farro, which sadly is not gluten-free. Back at home, I recreated the recipe using brown rice and it worked very well.

250 g (8 oz) brown rice
100 g (4 oz) cheese, such as feta or Cheddar, cut into cubes
50 g (2 oz) sun-dried tomatoes, chopped
50 g (2 oz) artichoke hearts, chopped
50 g (2 oz) salami or ham, cut into chunks

2–3 celery sticks, finely chopped
2–3 tsp capers (optional)
Flat leaf parsley, chopped

FOR THE DRESSING
4 tbsp olive oil
Freshly squeezed juice of ½ lemon
Salt and pepper

● Cook the rice as normal, but be careful not to overcook it – make sure it still has a little bite to it as the salad will not be a success with mushy rice! Rinse the rice with plenty of cold water and leave to drain well before making the salad.
● To prepare the dressing, whisk all the ingredients in a jar or small bowl. Season to taste.
● In a medium bowl combine the cheese, sun-dried tomatoes, artichokes, salami, celery and capers. Add the drained rice and

SNACKS

mix gently with a large spoon. Drizzle about half the dressing over the salad and mix gently. Taste and season again if necessary. Refrigerate until ready to serve.

● Just before serving, add the chopped parsley and drizzle a little more dressing over the salad and mix through.

Artichokes

 DON'T BE DAUNTED BY THE LIST OF INGREDIENTS. USE WHAT YOU'VE GOT AND LEAVE OUT ANYTHING YOU KNOW YOUR CHILDREN WON'T EAT.

IDEAL FOR A PICNIC!

Ruthie's Prawn Salad · SERVES 2–3

My daughter Ruthie loves this salad, especially the gherkins, so here's a salad for all the little gherkin–lovers out there.

225 g (7½ oz) freshly cooked king or tiger prawns, peeled and deveined
2 tbsp mayonnaise
1 tsp gluten-free wholegrain mustard
5–8 French cornichon (gherkins), diced

2 celery sticks, diced
1–2 tsp capers (optional)
Squeeze of fresh lemon juice
Tabasco sauce (optional)
Salt and freshly ground black pepper

● Dry the prawns with kitchen paper and cut into good-sized chunks. Add the mayonnaise, mustard, cornichons, celery, capers and salt and pepper to taste. Sharpen with a squeeze of lemon juice and Tabasco sauce. Chill until ready to use.

IT'S WORTH BUYING THE BIG JUICY PRAWNS AND NOT THE LITTLE FLUFFY THINGS THAT TASTE OF COTTON WOOL.

IF YOU BUY FRESH UNCOOKED PRAWNS, YOU WILL HAVE A TRULY SPECTACULAR DISH, BUT I KNOW THAT THIS IS EXPENSIVE AND TIME CONSUMING, SO USING READY PEELED, COOKED PRAWNS IS A GOOD ALTERNATIVE.

SNACKS

Tuna Salad (SERVES 1 GENEROUSLY)

This is a real workhouse salad in our family. It takes minutes to prepare and you can take it with you wherever you go. This salad has travelled across the Atlantic on lots of occasions and has even gone as far as South Africa.

85 g (3½ oz) can of tuna in brine
1 heaped tbsp mayonnaise
4–5 small gherkins, chopped
½ red pepper, seeded and
chopped

1 celery stick, chopped
Capers (optional)
A few tbsp canned sweetcorn
(optional)
Gluten-free crackers, to serve

● Drain the tuna and place in a bowl with all the other ingredients. Break up gently with a fork to combine everything. Serve with gluten-free crackers.

Nan's Chopped Salad

This is my friend Nançi's salad and it's a real winner. I am always amazed and delighted to see both my children polishing off an entire bowl of chopped raw vegetables. Here are a few suggestions but really the sky is the limit:

Carrots
Celery
Peppers (red, green, yellow)
Tomatoes
Radishes
Cabbage, finely sliced
Broccoli
Cauliflower
Red onion, finely chopped
Cucumber, peeled and diced

YOU CAN ALSO ADD
Cornichons, gherkins
Capers
Artichoke hearts
Olives
Pine nuts
Feta cheese
Ham/Chicken/Roast turkey/
Salami

● Use lots of raw vegetables, chopping them into even bite-sized chunks – anything goes.
● Dress the salad with a glug of good olive oil, a splash of balsamic vinegar, a squeeze of lemon juice, salt and pepper to taste.
● You can prepare the vegetables ahead of time but add the dressing just before serving as this will keep everything fresh and crunchy. Serve with wedges of hot Cornbread (page 98), Polenta Chips (page 64) or Cheesy Snakes (page 104) straight out of the oven. This also makes a great picnic salad – bring the dressing along in a separate container or jar, to add just before serving.

SNACKS

Chicken, Apricot and Pine Nut Salad SERVES 2–3

This is a good recipe to use when you've got some leftover roast chicken. You can easily scale up the recipe to serve a large crowd. Allow half a chicken breast per adult and a quarter of a chicken breast per child.

I cooked chicken breast, cut into chunks	A few leaves of crisp lettuce, shredded
4 dried apricots, chopped	Toasted pine nuts (optional)
A handful of raisins	Olive oil
	Salt

● Combine the chicken, apricots, raisins and lettuce in a bowl. Drizzle with a little olive oil, sprinkle with toasted pine nuts and sea salt. Toss lightly to combine.

To toast pine nuts: Heat a small non-stick skillet or frying pan until hot. Add the pine nuts and toast for a few minutes, shaking the pan a little. When the pine nuts are starting to turn golden they are ready. Sprinkle with a little sea salt.

Toasted Cheese Sandwiches

SERVES 2

I BOUGHT A SANDWICH MAKER ONLY TO FIND THAT THE CHILDREN PREFER THEM MADE IN A FRYING PAN.

Children love toasted cheese sandwiches. There is something so wonderfully comforting about them.

4 slices white gluten-free bread
Butter, softened
Cheese, such as Cheddar or Gruyère

1–2 tsp olive oil
Maldon sea salt (optional)

● Spread the butter evenly on both sides of the bread. Cut the cheese into thin slices and cover two slices of bread with cheese but don't overfill. Top with the remaining bread to make two sandwiches.

● Warm the oil in a small frying pan and when hot add one sandwich. Fry in the oil on moderate heat pressing down hard with a spatula. Flip onto the other side and repeat the process, pressing down hard to flatten the sandwich and melt the cheese. You shouldn't need to add more oil. If you add too much oil you may end up with a very greasy sandwich.

● When the sandwich is golden and the cheese is melted remove from the pan. Sprinkle with a tiny bit of Maldon sea salt and cut on the diagonal. Repeat with the remaining sandwich. Serve immediately.

Variation: You can add thin slices of ham or turkey with the cheese.

YOU DON'T NEED A SPECIAL BIT OF EQUIPMENT TO MAKE THESE.

SNACKS

TACOS DON'T LIKE TO SIT AROUND, SO PREPARE ALL THE FILLINGS IN ADVANCE AND THEN ASSEMBLE THEM AT THE LAST MINUTE.

Tacos

Filled tacos make a delicious gluten-free snack and there is no limit to the fillings or combinations you can use. Kids love making them, so sometimes I just set out bowls with different fillings and let them do their own thing. Here are a few of our favourite fillings. Allow at least two tacos per person.

CLASSIC MEXICAN TACOS
Gluten-free Corn tacos
Grated cheese
Shredded lettuce
Chopped tomatoes
Cubes of avocado
Refried beans (gluten-free)
Ready-made gluten-free salsa

ALL-DAY BREAKFAST TACOS
Scrambled eggs
Cubes of gluten-free sausages
or bacon
Ready-made gluten-free salsa

CALIFORNIA TACOS
Shredded cooked chicken
Alfalfa sprouts or mustard cress
Cubes of avocado
Chopped tomatoes
Pesto mayonnaise dressing
(combine 1 tsp of pesto with
2 tsp mayonnaise and a little
freshly squeezed lemon juice)

BEACH HOUSE TACOS
Ruthie's Prawn salad
(see page 120)
Shredded lettuce
Chopped tomatoes

● Pre-heat the oven to 180°C (350°F) Gas 4. Warm the tacos in the oven for 5 minutes to crisp up. Fill and serve.
Note: Tacos make good picnic fare. Take along a range of fillings in different containers. You can also use plain tortilla chips instead of tacos.

LUNCH AND LIGHT

Crêpes (MAKES ABOUT 20 CRÊPES)

YOU CAN MAKE YOUR CRÊPES AND FILL THEM IN ADVANCE.

Crêpes are great – they are so versatile, quick and filling. You can make very good gluten-free crêpes that will be popular for lunch or supper. Crêpes freeze well. I tend to make a batch and keep back a few as standbys in the freezer.

150 g (5 oz) gluten-free
plain flour
50 g (2 oz) buckwheat flour
A pinch of salt
1 tsp sugar
2 eggs

410 ml (14½ fl oz) milk
125 ml (4 fl oz) water
1 tbsp butter, melted
Butter
Sunflower oil

● In a medium bowl combine the flour, buckwheat flour, salt and sugar. In a separate bowl lightly beat the eggs and combine with the milk and water. Add the liquid slowly to the flour mixture to make a smooth batter. Don't worry too much about lumps as these will dissolve as the batter is left to stand.

● Leave the batter to stand for about 20 minutes. Stir and add the melted butter. The batter should be the consistency of single cream. If it is a bit too thick add a little more water.

● In the meantime, cut out squares of greaseproof paper. You will need about 20, 15 cm (6 in) squares.

● Melt some butter and oil in a small frying pan, with a diameter of approximately 15 cm (6 in). Heat until hot and pour out any excess oil. Add a spoonful of batter and swirl to completely cover the pan. Remove any excess batter. Cook until the edges start to

SNACKS

☆ THEY WILL KEEP IN THE FRIDGE FOR SEVERAL HOURS WITHOUT ANY PROBLEM.

☆ JUST POP THEM IN THE OVEN FOR 10–15 MINUTES TO HEAT THROUGH.

curl away from the side of the pan. Flip the crêpe onto the other side and cook for a few more seconds.

● Repeat the process until you have used up all the batter. As each crêpe is ready, place on a greaseproof square. Continue layering the crêpes with sheets of greaseproof paper in between until all the batter has been used. Keep the crêpes warm in a low oven.

To freeze crêpes

● If you are planning to freeze the crêpes, allow them to cool completely. Then put them in a container (with their greaseproof paper dividers), a tight-fitting lid and freeze. Allow them to defrost for 10–15 minutes before using.

To assemble crêpes

● Pre-heat the oven to 180°C (350°F) Gas 4.

● If you are using your crêpes straight away then prepare your filling. Really anything goes with crêpes. Use your imagination and make use of any leftovers in the fridge. Some suggestions include mushroom and bacon, ham, cheddar and tomato, or ricotta and fresh herbs.

● Place a spoonful of filling in the middle of the crêpe. Fold the crêpe in half to make a half moon. Then fold the crêpe in half again to make a triangle. Try not to overfill the crêpes as the filling will all ooze out when they are in the oven. Place your filled crêpes in a baking dish and bake in a hot oven for 10 minutes.

Note: Drizzle with Roast Tomato Sauce (see page 134).

LUNCH AND LIGHT

Lunch Boxes and Picnics

I really enjoy putting a lunch box or picnic together. I love the challenge of it and surprising the children. I've made use of the recipes in the cookbook to put some ideas together, but I too rely on pre-packed supermarket treats, like yoghurts, crisps, chocolate bars and biscuits for filling in when time is short.

Here are a few lunch box tips
- Salad and soups can be made the day or night before
- Leftovers make great lunch box food
- Keep a selection of breads and savouries pre-packed in the freezer
- Keep a stash of cookies, muffins and breads pre-packed in the freezer
- Pack crudités and fresh fruit in small plastic bags to save space
- Purchase containers with tight-fitting lids that won't leak

Snacks on the go
We never leave the house without a lunch box. Eating out is just too unpredictable and there is nothing worse than dragging a hungry child around. Although things are improving, finding something healthy and gluten-free at short notice is not always possible. I am always prepared with a few snacks up my sleeve:

- Gluten-free crackers with peanut butter, marmite or butter
- Rice cakes with butter and honey
- Slices of red pepper, celery, cherry tomatoes
- Fresh fruit
- Cheese cut into cubes or wands
- Salami, ham, turkey
- Smoked salmon
- Olives
- Pickles
- Hummus

SNACKS

KEEP A SELECTION OF ICE PACKS IN YOUR FREEZER.

BUY A GOOD WIDE-MOUTHED THERMOS THAT WILL HOLD HOT FOOD, SUCH AS SOUPS.

A Few Lunchbox and Picnic Ideas

Pasta Salad (page 117)
Fresh fruit (apples, blueberries, mango, banana)
Chocolate Chip Cookies (page 68)

~☆~

Rice Salad (page 118)
Gluten–free Breadsticks (page 200)
Marble Cake (page 170)

~☆~

Tuna Salad (page 121)
Cheesy Snakes (page 104)
Tropical Rice Crispy Bars (page 187)

~☆~

Lucia's Bean Soup (page 116)
Gluten–free Breadsticks (page 200)
Fresh fruit

Crispy Chicken Nuggets (page 56)
Guacamole Dip (page 196)
Carrot and Raisin Salad (page 159)
Brownies (page 180)

~☆~

Cornbread (page 98)
Creamy Tomato Soup (page 112)
Apple Hazelnut Loaf (page 164)

~☆~

Chilli con Carne (page 146)
Tortilla chips
Dalia's Luscious Lemon Bars (page 184)

~☆~

Nan's Chopped Salad (page 122)
Polenta Chips (page 64)
Peanut Butter Cookies (page 178)

tea time

What to have for tea? For many of you out there, this thought enters your mind around 3.30 p.m. just as you are collecting the children from school. And then the inevitable feeling of panic sets in. This fear is doubled when you know you cannot rely on ready-made meals or sauces from the supermarket, as most of these contain gluten. Do not panic. In the following chapter you will find many delicious, healthy and often very quick recipes for tea time. All of these recipes are child-friendly and many of these meals can be prepared in less than half an hour.

Tea Time

I cannot stress enough the importance of sitting down with your children and having a meal together. I know that this is not always possible, but I do urge you to make this the exception and not the rule. Conversation and good food make for such a good atmosphere.

I've included a family menu planner at the back of the book to help guide you through the week. If you can, sit down at the weekend and select some dishes for the following week and make your shopping list as you go along.

There are also many recipes in this chapter which you can freeze, in small batches, for days when planning has gone out of the window.

See also
- Shepherd's Pie, page 54
- Crispy Chicken Nuggets, page 56
- Macaroni and Cheese, page 62
- Deborah's Delicious Meatballs, page 58
- Fish Fingers, page 60
- Polenta Chips, page 64

DELICIOUS FOOD!

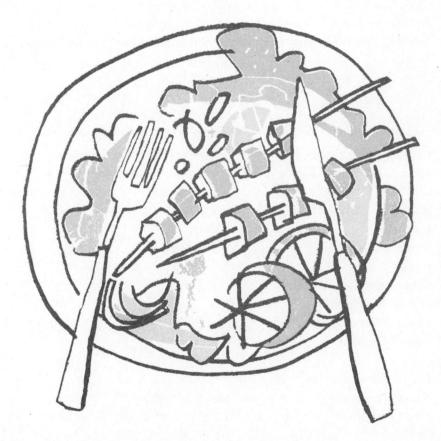

TEA TIME

Yummy Meatloaf and Roast Tomato Sauce SERVES 4–6

This is real comfort food. It's easy to make and kids love the soft texture. It's worth tracking down a good butcher who can supply organic pork and veal for this recipe. The sauce is a good all-rounder: use it as a base for a rich tomato soup; a quick pasta sauce or serve with crêpes.

2 tbsp butter
1 onion, finely chopped
500 g (1 lb) ground lean veal or beef
500 g (1 lb) ground lean pork
1 large apple, peeled, cored and grated
1 egg
3 slices gluten-free bread, soaked in milk
1 sprig of fresh rosemary
Salt and pepper

FOR ROAST TOMATO SAUCE
Tomatoes (2 punnets cherry tomatoes or 8 standard size tomatoes)
2–3 garlic cloves
Olive oil
Sea salt
Freshly squeezed juice of ½ lemon

● Pre-heat the oven to 220°C (425°F) Gas 7.
● Melt the butter in a saucepan and add the onion. Cook until the onions are soft and transparent but not brown. Sprinkle a bit of salt on them and leave to cool.
● Combine the veal and pork in a large bowl. Add the grated

COMFORT FOOD

YOU CAN MAKE THE SAUCE AHEAD OF TIME OR WHEN YOU HAVE A GLUT OF TOMATOES THAT NEED TO BE USED UP.

apple, egg, soaked bread and cooked onions. Season. Pack the mixture into a loaf tin measuring 23 x 13 cm (9 x 5 in). Press the sprig of rosemary into the centre of the loaf, obscuring most of it. Bake in a hot oven for about 40 minutes.

● To test if the meatloaf is cooked, insert a thin knife into the middle and leave for 10 seconds. Remove and test the tip of the knife on the inside of your wrist. It should feel very hot! Remove the sprig of rosemary before serving. Serve with roast tomato sauce, mashed potatoes and a bowl of salad.

To make the tomato sauce

● Rinse the tomatoes in cool water. If you are using cherry tomatoes, shake off the excess water and place them in a roasting tin. If you are using larger tomatoes, cut them in half and place them cut side down in the roasting tin. Scatter the garlic cloves amongst the tomatoes, then drizzle with olive oil and sprinkle with sea salt. Add the lemon juice. Roast in a hot oven until the skins are blistering and slightly charred. This usually takes about 30 minutes.

● Remove from the oven and place the contents in a metal sieve with a bowl underneath to catch the juice. Push the mixture through the sieve until all you have left is dry pulp, seeds and skins. This takes a bit of elbow grease, but I promise it will be worth it. If the sauce seems a bit thin place it in a small saucepan and reduce to a better consistency. Check the seasoning and adjust accordingly.

Sticky Ribs SERVES 4

ONE OF MY RECIPE TESTERS TRIED THIS WITH CHICKEN DRUMSTICKS AND SAID IT WORKED BEAUTIFULLY. YOU MAY NEED TO DECREASE THE COOKING TIME SLIGHTLY.

Gluten-free generally rules out Chinese food, as soy sauce is a big no-no. This recipe, adapted from Madhur Jaffrey's *Far Eastern Cookery*, is an easy way to cook home-made Chinese-style ribs and the results are delicious.

1 kg (2 lb) pork spare ribs, cut into 8–10 cm (3–4 in) pieces
6 tbsp gluten-free soy sauce
3 tbsp dark brown sugar

3 tbsp caster sugar
3 x 4 cm (1½ in) cubes of fresh root ginger, peeled and smashed

● Put the meat in a large pot. Add the soy sauce, sugars and the smashed cubes of ginger and pour in enough water to just cover the meat. Bring to the boil and then lower the heat so that the meat simmers gently. Skim off any scum that comes to the surface. Cover and cook the meat over a medium heat for about 25 minutes.
● Remove the ginger cubes. Turn the heat up high, remove the lid and boil vigorously until almost all the liquid is reduced and you are left with a sticky syrup. You will need to turn the ribs during this time to make sure they coat evenly. This part of the cooking can take another 20 minutes or longer and when you look inside the pot, you may think it is all going horribly wrong! It's not. Just be patient and allow the liquid to reduce. Towards the end, just be careful the sauce doesn't scorch.
● When the ribs look glossy, shiny and sticky, take them out. Put them in a serving dish and pour the remaining sauce over them. Serve with sticky white rice.

REALLY TASTY!

TRY USING CHICKEN BREASTS INSTEAD OF PORK.

Polenta and Cumin Pork Chops

SERVES 4

This quick recipe is really tasty. The coating gives the chops a soft, slightly crispy texture. Serve with rice and hot buttered carrots. Use the best quality pork you can find.

50 g (2 oz) polenta
50 g (2 oz) gluten-free plain flour
1 tbsp ground cumin
4 pork chops on the bone

Olive oil
Sunflower oil
Salt and pepper

- Pre-heat the oven to 180°C (350°F) Gas 4.
- Put the polenta, flour, cumin, salt and pepper in a large, clean plastic bag and mix to combine the flour and spices. Add the pork chops, shaking the bag vigorously to make sure they are well coated. Shake off any excess flour and leave the chops on a tray for a few minutes.
- Meanwhile, heat a few tablespoons of olive oil and sunflower oil in a sturdy frying pan, large enough to hold all the chops (if you haven't got a big enough pan, then do them in batches). Make sure the oil is quite hot before placing the pork chops in the pan. Fry for a few minutes on one side until golden and then flip over and fry them on the other side.
- When nicely golden on both sides, place them in a large roasting tin and put them in the oven for about 10–15 minutes. The pork should be firm and not at all pink. Serve immediately.

Chicken and Vegetable Curry

SERVES 4–6

This is a great dish because it's quick, versatile and tasty – you can add anything you like to the sauce. I've made it very mild, but you can play around with the heat, depending on taste.

FOR THE SAUCE
2 tbsp sunflower oil
1 medium onion, sliced
2.5 cm (1 in) piece of fresh ginger root, peeled and finely chopped
2 garlic cloves, finely chopped
1 fresh chilli, deseeded (optional)
1 bay leaf
2 tsp garam masala
1 tsp mild curry powder
400 ml (14 fl oz) can coconut milk
500 ml (17 fl oz) chicken stock
Salt and pepper

FOR THE VEGETABLES AND MEAT
2 medium potatoes, peeled and diced
2 carrots, peeled and cut into chunks
A handful of broccoli florets
A handful of cauliflower florets
2 small courgettes, peeled and diced
3 skinless chicken breast fillets, cut into large chunks

YOU CAN MAKE THE SAUCE AHEAD OF TIME – IT WILL SIT HAPPILY IN THE FRIDGE FOR A FEW DAYS.

PACKED WITH VEG ♡ ♡

● In a medium saucepan soften the onion in the sunflower oil until translucent and season. Add the ginger and garlic and cook until fragrant. Add the garam masala and the curry powder and fry for another minute or so. Pour in the coconut milk and the chicken stock and add the chilli and bay leaf. Cover and simmer the sauce on a low heat for about 15 minutes.

● Meanwhile, prepare the vegetables, peeling, dicing and cutting them into good-sized chunks. When the sauce is ready, begin by adding the vegetables that require the longest cooking time, such as the potatoes and carrots. Cook for 10 minutes, then add the softer vegetables, like the broccoli and cauliflower, and the chicken. Cook for a further 10 minutes. Finally, add the courgettes and cook for about 5 minutes. Check the seasoning and adjust accordingly. Serve with plain basmati rice.

Variation: You can substitute fish or prawns for the chicken or just add more vegetables to make a vegetarian curry.

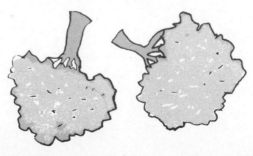

Chicken Pot Pie SERVES 4–6

This is a good Sunday lunch dish, which is packed full of vegetables. Use the best quality chicken you can find and serve this with steamed broccoli or any other green vegetable.

4 skinless chicken breast fillets, about 500 g (1 lb)
50 g (2 oz) cornflour
5–6 tbsp sunflower oil
75 g (3 oz) butter
3 leeks, finely sliced
3–4 celery sticks, finely chopped
2 carrots, peeled and finely diced
200 ml (7 fl oz) gluten-free chicken stock

1 bay leaf
1 tsp gluten-free mustard
2 handfuls of petite pois or peas (fresh or frozen)
4 medium potatoes, about 600–700 g (1¼–1½ lb), peeled
Milk
Freshly grated Parmesan cheese (optional)
Salt and pepper

● Cut each breast fillet into 8 pieces. Try to keep the pieces equal in size so that they cook evenly.
● Place the cornflour in a plastic bag or in a bowl and season with salt and pepper. Add the chicken pieces and cover liberally with flour. Shake off any excess and place the chicken pieces on a piece of kitchen paper.
● Heat the oil in a large frying pan and add the chicken in batches. Do not overcrowd the pan as you want the chicken to brown evenly. Turn each piece and brown evenly on each side. Once brown, remove and place in an ovenproof dish.

GOOD FOR SUNDAY LUNCH

- Wipe the frying pan with a paper towel and melt 25 g (1 oz) of the butter. Add the leeks and fry gently. Next, add the celery and after a few minutes, the diced carrots. Cook for a few minutes then add the chicken stock and the bay leaf. Simmer gently until the carrots are just tender. Add the mustard and adjust the seasoning. Combine the chicken and vegetables and add the peas. Bring the mixture up to simmering again and then remove from the heat. Pour this mixture into the ovenproof dish.
- Pre-heat the oven to 180°C (350°F) Gas 4.
- Now prepare the topping. Cut each potato into 6 even-sized chunks. Place in a saucepan with cold water and bring to the boil. Boil until the potatoes are just tender, then drain. Add 25–50 g (1–2 oz) of butter, a dash of milk and seasoning, then mash the potato.
- Evenly dollop the mashed potato on top of the chicken. Make sure the chicken is well covered, but leave it a bit rough and ready, so that it will crisp up a little in the oven. Sprinkle with grated Parmesan and put in the oven. Bake for 40–45 minutes, until bubbling hot.

Note: For a slightly speedier version, you can poach whole chicken breasts until just cooked and then chop them into chunks. Add the chicken to the cooked vegetables and proceed as per the recipe.

Enchilada Pie SERVES 4-6

This is an unusual supper dish, one which older children will enjoy. You can purchase ready-made gluten-free corn tortillas from the Cool Chile Co.

4 tbsp sunflower oil
1 medium onion, chopped
2 garlic cloves, chopped
500 g (1 lb) minced beef
225 g (7½ oz) jar gluten-free salsa
2 tsp dried oregano
1 tsp mild chilli powder
2 tsp ground cumin
150 g (5 oz) frozen or fresh sweetcorn

1 tbsp butter
1 red or green pepper, cored and finely sliced
12 gluten-free corn tortillas, 15 cm (6 in) in diameter
275 ml (9 fl oz) soured cream
200 g (7 oz) grated Cheddar cheese
50 g (2 oz) black olives, pitted and sliced
Salt and pepper

● Warm the oil in a large pan. Add the onion and cook until translucent. Add the garlic and fry for a few minutes until fragrant. Add the minced beef and break up with a wooden spoon until no longer pink. Add the salsa, oregano, chilli powder and cumin, salt and pepper. Mix well and cook over medium heat, covered, for 5–10 minutes. Add a little water if the mixture is a bit dry.

MEXICAN FOOD

● While the meat is cooking, melt the butter in a small pan. Add the pepper and stir fry until just wilted. Add the sweetcorn and stir fry for a few more minutes.

● Pre-heat the oven to 180°C (350°F) Gas 4.

● Line the bottom of an ovenproof dish with a layer of tortillas. Then add a layer of meat, a layer of grated cheese and finally soured cream. Repeat to add two more layers. Sprinkle the pepper and corn mixture on the top along with the olives. Bake for 30–40 minutes until hot and bubbly. Serve with a green salad.

Peppers

YOU CAN PURCHASE A TORTILLA PRESS AND SPECIAL MAIZE FLOUR (MASA HARINA) FROM THE COOL CHILE CO.

Chicken Kebabs with Peanut Sauce `SERVES 4`

Inspired by one of my favourite cookery books, *Crazy Water, Pickled Lemons* by Diana Henry, this recipe is great for a summer barbeque. Any leftovers also make great picnic food.

500 g (1 lb) chicken breast or thigh fillets, cut into chunks

FOR THE MARINADE
100 ml (3½ fl oz) natural yoghurt
3 small garlic cloves, peeled and squashed
½ tsp ground cinnamon
¼ tsp cayenne pepper (optional)
Freshly squeezed juice of ½ lemon
Freshly squeezed juice of ½ lime
5 cm (2 in) cube of fresh root ginger, peeled and smashed

FOR THE PEANUT SAUCE
2 tbsp sunflower oil
1 shallot, finely sliced
2 garlic cloves, finely chopped
½ tsp chilli powder
½ tsp salt
125 g (4½ oz) crunchy peanut butter
2 tsp dark brown sugar
Freshly squeezed lime juice

FOR THE CRUNCHY SALAD
½ cucumber
2 red peppers
1 pack of sugar snap peas (about 15–20)
Freshly chopped herbs (mint, coriander, parsley)

SUMMER ☆ BARBEQUE ☆

● First, prepare the marinade. In a bowl combine the yoghurt, garlic, cinnamon, cayenne pepper, lemon and lime juice and the ginger. Mix with a spoon. Pour the marinade over the chicken and leave to marinate for a minimum of 3 hours. If possible, marinate the chicken overnight.

● Make the peanut sauce. Heat the oil in a small frying pan, then add the shallot and cook gently until soft. Add the garlic, chilli powder and salt and fry until just golden and fragrant. Pour the onion–garlic mixture into a small saucepan and add 100 ml (3½ fl oz) water and the peanut butter. Cook the mixture over a gentle heat for about 15 minutes. If it is too thick add a little more water. Add the sugar and lime juice. Allow to cool before serving.

● Make the kebabs. Remove the chicken from the fridge at least an hour before cooking. If using wooden skewers, soak them in hot water for 5–10 minutes. Heat the grill until it's really hot. In the meantime, skewer the chicken fillets. Place them on the hot grill, turning them as necessary. Check they are thoroughly cooked through before serving.

● Just before serving prepare the salad. Peel and deseed the cucumber. Cut into chunks. Deseed the peppers and slice. Remove any threads and top and tail the sugar snap peas. Cut each sugar snap into 2 or 3 pieces. Arrange the salad on a large plate. Sprinkle with lime juice and then top with the freshly chopped herbs.

Chilli con Carne SERVES 4

This is a hearty dish, which children enjoy, despite all the veggies hidden inside. Serve with plain rice, crispy tortilla chips and bowls of grated cheese, soured cream and lime wedges.

500 g (1 lb) lean minced beef
2 tbsp olive oil
1 medium onion, chopped
1 green pepper, diced
3–4 celery sticks, finely chopped
2 garlic cloves, finely chopped
1 tbsp dried oregano
1 tsp ground coriander
2 tsp ground cumin

2 tbsp mild chilli powder
2 bay leaves
300 ml (½ pint) gluten-free chicken stock
1 gluten-free bouillon stock cube
400 g (13 oz) can tomatoes
3 heaped tsp tomato purée
400 g (13 oz) can kidney beans, rinsed and drained

● Heat the oil in a heavy saucepan over high heat. Add the minced beef, breaking it down with a wooden spoon. Cook for about 5 minutes. Add the onion, pepper, celery and garlic and continue cooking for another 5 minutes. Add all the herbs and spices and cook through so that the spices are fragrant. Continue to stir so that it doesn't catch and burn. Add the chicken stock, stock cube, tomatoes and tomato purée and bring to a simmer.
● Turn the heat to low, cover and simmer for about 30–40 minutes, stirring occasionally. If the mixture looks a little dry, add a bit of water and continue cooking.
● Before serving add the kidney beans. Gently simmer for 5 minutes.

YOU WILL NOTICE THAT THE MEASUREMENTS ARE DECIDEDLY VAGUE.

 THAT'S BECAUSE IT IS A VERY FORGIVING DISH AND YOU CAN REALLY MAKE IT UP AS YOU GO ALONG. IT WILL STILL TASTE GREAT.

Nan's Seafood Pot   SERVES 4

There are so many good things about this dish that I will have to limit myself to telling you about three. First, it's really quick to make – 15 minutes start to finish. Second, most of the ingredients are kept in your freezer. Third, it is light, delicious and healthy.

2 medium onions, finely chopped
Olive oil
2 spring onions, finely sliced, including green tops
3 celery sticks and celery leaf, finely chopped
3 garlic cloves, finely chopped
250 ml (8 fl oz) white wine
2 tbsp Thai fish sauce
White pepper

400–600 g large frozen peeled prawns
625 g (1 ¼ lb) frozen white fish (such as haddock or cod)
Frozen peas
Frozen soya beans
Fresh coriander, finely chopped
Chilli flakes, to garnish (optional)
Lemon, to garnish

● Prepare sufficient white or brown rice for 4 people.
● Gently fry the onion in the oil until soft and translucent. Add the spring onion, celery, celery leaf and garlic and fry for a few minutes until fragrant. Add the white wine, fish sauce and white pepper and simmer for 5 minutes.
● Next, add the prawns, fish, peas and soya beans. Cook for 2–3 minutes until the vegetables and fish and prawns are just cooked. Taste and season accordingly. Serve in bowls over freshly cooked rice and garnish with coriander, lemon and chilli flakes.

Sarah Fishburn's Fish Bake SERVES 4

This is a lovely recipe for a cold autumn or winter evening. It's hearty, rich and comforting and you can have supper on the table in 35 minutes, start to finish. I am truly grateful to Sarah for sharing it.

4–6 fillets of mixed fish (a combination of white fish and salmon works well), fresh or frozen
I pack of frozen prawns, about 200 g (7 oz)

8–10 ripe cherry tomatoes
150 ml (¼ pint) double cream
150 g (5 oz) grated mature Cheddar cheese
Fresh basil
Salt and pepper

● Select an ovenproof dish. A ceramic dish works well but the cooking time may be a bit longer. If you have a cast iron ovenproof skillet or a Le Creuset baking dish the cooking time will be greatly reduced.
● Pre-heat the oven to 220°C (425°F) Gas 7.
● Place the fish fillets in the dish. Top with the frozen prawns. Slice the tomatoes in half and scatter around the dish. Season with salt and pepper. Pour the cream over the top and add the grated Cheddar.
● Put the dish in the pre-heated oven and bake for 25–35 minutes, until bubbly and golden. The cooking time will depend on the thickness of the fillets and the type of dish used.

YUMMY! ☆

Kung Po Prawn Stir Fry SERVES 4

This yummy stir fry tastes very authentic – the sort of thing you would get from the local Chinese takeaway only a million miles better. You can also substitute beef or chicken for the prawns.

50 ml (2 fl oz) orange juice
3 tbsp red wine vinegar
1½ tbsp gluten-free soy sauce
1 tbsp sugar
1 tsp cornflour
2 tbsp sunflower oil
1 medium onion, chopped
into large chunks
1½ tsp finely minced fresh
root ginger

2 garlic cloves, finely minced
1 red pepper, deseeded and
chopped into large dice
400 g (13 oz) peeled raw prawns
A handful of roasted cashews,
chopped (optional)
Toasted sesame oil
½ tsp salt

● In a small bowl combine the orange juice, vinegar, soy sauce, sugar and cornflour.
● Heat the oil in a large frying pan or wok. When hot, add the onion and stir fry for a minute. Add the ginger and stir fry, then the garlic. Stir fry for another minute until fragrant. Add the red pepper and stir through. Add the prawns and stir fry for one and a half minutes until just pink.
● Add the soy sauce mixture and stir. The mixture will thicken slightly. If it's too thick add a little water to thin out. Stir in the chopped cashews and sprinkle with a little sesame oil. Serve over plain boiled rice.

Torta de Mazorca SERVES 8–12

This recipe for a savoury corn pudding comes from my aunt Ruthie. It can be served as a main course with a salad or as a vegetable dish with a meat course.

10 corn cobs (see note)
6 tbsp sugar
½ tsp salt

100 g (4 oz) mild Cheddar cheese, grated
6 eggs, well beaten
2–3 tbsp polenta (optional)

● Pre-heat the oven to 180°C (350°F) Gas 4. Grease a 33 x 23 cm (13 x 9 in) ovenproof dish.

● With a sharp knife, cut the corn off the cobs and place in a bowl. With a hand-held blender or food processor, blend the corn until mushy. Add the sugar, salt, cheese and the eggs. If the mixture is very runny, add 2–3 tablespoons of polenta, until the consistency is like cake mixture. Mix all the ingredients and pour into the prepared ovenproof dish. Bake for about 45 minutes until set and lightly golden brown. Serve warm.

● Any leftovers can be parcelled up in tin foil and put in the freezer. To reheat, place the parcel (direct from the freezer) in a hot oven 200°C (400°F) Gas 6, for 15–20 minutes until hot.

Note: Substitute the corn with 1kg (2 lb) of frozen corn. The texture is not the same but it still tastes terrific. Thaw the corn by rinsing it in boiling water for a few seconds. Then proceed as per the recipe.

SERVE WITH NAN'S CHOPPED
SALAD (PAGE 122) FOR A
MEGA HEALTHY MEAL

Vegetable Bake *SERVES 4*

This tasty dish takes a bit of time to prepare but then you put it in the oven and forget about it. You can substitute different vegetables according to taste or the seasons. All vegetables should be peeled and thinly sliced.

50–75 g (2–3 oz) butter, melted
2 large potatoes
1 tsp dried thyme or oregano
1 medium butternut squash
3 medium courgettes

250 ml (8 fl oz) passata
1 garlic clove
Parmesan or Cheddar cheese, grated
Salt and pepper

● Pre-heat the oven to 180°C (350°F) Gas 4. Grease an ovenproof dish with a little melted butter.

● Place a layer of potatoes at the bottom of the dish. Drizzle with butter and then season with salt and pepper and sprinkle with a little thyme. Repeat with the butternut squash and the courgettes. Press down slightly. Cover with a thin layer of passata. Scatter slices of garlic around the top and season.

● Cover the dish with foil and bake for approximately 1½ hours. The thinner the vegetables the quicker the cooking time. At this point, either leave to cool or proceed with the topping. The vegetables will keep overnight refrigerated. When you are ready to serve, add the grated cheese and bake for 10–15 minutes until the cheese is melted and bubbling hot.

Chinese Fried Rice *SERVES 4*

This is a good Sunday evening supper dish that you can adapt according to what you have in the fridge. If you have some leftover rice, then this is the time to use it up. Try adding strips of red pepper and frozen peas for extra crunch and colour.

2 tbsp sunflower oil
1 large onion, finely sliced
5 rashers of bacon or pancetta, cut into small pieces
A handful of raisins

125 g (4½ oz) tinned sweetcorn
Cooked rice for 4
Gluten-free soy sauce or Tamari sauce (optional)

● In a large frying pan warm the oil and add the onion. Cook over a medium heat until the onion is softened and translucent. Add the bacon and cook until the bacon and onion are slightly caramelised but not burned. Stir in the raisins and sweetcorn and cook for a few more minutes.

● Finally, add the cooked rice, stirring through with a fork or a spatula so as not to break up the rice too much. Cook until the rice is piping hot. Season with salt and pepper. Serve immediately and allow each person to add soy sauce to taste.

RICE THINGS ☆

Chickeny Rice SERVES 2–3

I borrowed this idea from my brother-in-law Scott. My children love this when they are feeling a bit under the weather or when they just want a comforting supper. It is also great for breakfast when it's cold and damp outside.

125 g (4½ oz) basmati rice
2 tsp concentrated liquid
gluten-free chicken stock

25 g (1 oz) butter
Parmesan cheese, grated
Salt and pepper

● Rinse the rice in water a few times to release some of the starch, then put it in a saucepan with 400 ml (14 fl oz) water. Bring just to the boil and add the chicken stock and butter. Turn the heat down to low and cover the pan.

● Cook for 10 minutes or until the rice is just soft. Taste and season with salt and pepper. Serve in bowls topped with Parmesan cheese.

Pad Thai *SERVES 4*

This recipe came about from some testing that went horribly wrong. It just goes to prove that good things can come from cooking disasters. The sweet and peanuty flavours will be popular with children, especially if you give them some chopsticks.

FOR THE PAD THAI
1–2 tbsp sunflower oil
250 g (8 oz) uncooked rice noodles
50 ml (2 fl oz) gluten-free sweet chilli sauce
2–3 tbsp gluten-free tomato ketchup
1 egg, lightly beaten
Freshly squeezed lime juice

FOR THE PEANUT SAUCE
1 tbsp sunflower oil
1 shallot, finely sliced
3 large spoonfuls crunchy peanut butter
100 ml (3½ fl oz) gluten–free chicken stock
1 tsp light brown sugar
Salt

TO SERVE
Freshly chopped coriander
Lime wedges

● First, make the peanut sauce. Heat the oil in a small saucepan and add the shallot and cook until soft and translucent. Add the peanut butter and the chicken stock and cook over a medium heat for a few minutes until the sauce is the consistency of thick double cream. Add sugar and salt to taste. Set aside. The sauce can be made several days in advance and kept in the refrigerator.
● To cook the noodles, follow the instructions on the packet.

PEANUTY ♡ ♡ ☆ NOODLES

Generally the noodles go into boiling water with a drop of oil. Stir the noodles to prevent them sticking and bring the water back up to the boil. Turn off the heat and leave the noodles for 3 minutes. Drain. Immediately add the peanut sauce and mix through. The noodles and peanut sauce will sit happily in the fridge for up to 24 hours.

● When you are ready to make the Pad Thai, heat the oil in a large wok. When it is hot, add the noodles with peanut sauce and stir through for one minute. Add the chilli sauce, ketchup and egg and stir fry for another minute until the egg is cooked through. Add the lime juice at the end.

● Serve in bowls sprinkled with freshly chopped coriander and wedges of lime.

Pasta à la Mama `SERVES 2`

This is a good standby when the cupboard is bare. Use the best bacon you can find – I prefer Italian pancetta because it's deliciously smoky without being too salty. You can make the sauce while the pasta is cooking.

Gluten-free pasta, for 2
1 tbsp olive oil
1 tbsp butter
1 medium onion, finely sliced
1 garlic clove, chopped

3–4 slices pancetta or good quality bacon, cut into fine strips
gluten-free chicken stock or water
100 g (4 oz) frozen peas
Parmesan cheese, grated

● Put the water on to boil for the pasta. Add the pasta.
● Meanwhile, in a small frying pan melt the butter and olive oil, and sweat the onion until translucent and soft, but do not allow to colour. Add the garlic and bacon and fry for a few minutes. Season with a little salt and pepper. Add a little bit of water from the pasta or some chicken stock to make a sauce and then add the peas. Cook for a few more minutes adding more liquid if necessary.
● Cook the pasta until al dente, then drain and mix with the sauce, Sprinkle with grated Parmesan and serve immediately.

QUICK CARROTS

Carrots à la Ewelme SERVES 4

The name of these delicious carrots comes from honey given to us by Jane Smale, who keeps bees in a little village in Oxfordshire. The connection with this beautiful place and Jane's wonderful honey makes them rather special, but in fact any good honey will do the trick.

4–5 medium carrots, peeled and cut into batons
Still mineral water (see note)

A good knob of butter
1 heaped tsp honey (clear or set)
Salt and pepper

● Place the carrots in a medium saucepan. Add enough water to just cover the carrots. Cook the carrots over a medium heat until just tender, then raise the heat and boil rapidly to reduce some of the liquid. You want some liquid in the pan to avoid burning the carrots but not a lot.

● Add the butter, honey and seasoning. Stir through to coat and cook until just glossy and a tiny bit syrupy. Serve with Polenta and Cumin Pork Chops (see page 137).

Note: Ordinary tap water can sometimes have a chemical taste. Filtered water would be okay to use instead.

Crunchy Creamy Coleslaw SERVES 4–6

Here's a quick coleslaw that has lots of flavour and is not overpowered by mayonnaise. Serve this in the summer with barbequed meats, burgers or chicken kebabs. In the winter, it's great with fish fingers or grilled chicken.

500 g (1 lb) red or white cabbage
2 carrots, peeled

FOR THE DRESSING
5 tsp mayonnaise
6–8 French cornichon (gherkins), chopped
Freshly squeezed juice of ½ lime
1 tsp Dijon mustard
1 tsp sugar
Rice vinegar

● Slice the cabbage finely or, better still, do it quickly in a food processor. Place the shredded cabbage in a large bowl. Coarsely grate the carrots and mix with the cabbage.

● To make the dressing, combine all of the ingredients in a glass jar with a lid. Shake to mix. Add the dressing to the cabbage and carrots and mix gently using two forks. Serve immediately.

GREAT FOR PICNICS AND BBQ'S

BARBEQUES

Carrot and Raisin Salad *SERVES 2*

Young children really like this salad, partly because it's messy to eat and the raisins make it sweet and crunchy. It's nice to serve this with fish fingers or chicken nuggets.

2 medium carrots, peeled
A small handful of seedless
raisins

Mayonnaise
Rice vinegar
Salt

● Shred the carrots on a coarse grater and place in a bowl. Add the raisins and just enough mayonnaise to hold it together, usually about a tablespoon. Don't overdo it, you can always add more if you want, but you don't want the carrots completely drowned in mayonnaise. Add a little splash of rice vinegar and a sprinkle of salt.

carrots

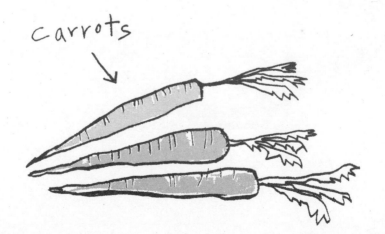

GLUTEN-FREE BROWNIES, CRUNCHY BISCOTTI, DELICIOUS MOIST CAKES.

Marble cake

LUSCIOUS LEMON BARS...THEY ARE ALL POSSIBLE.

SEE ALSO SHRIMPY'S CHOCOLATE CAKE, PAGE 70 PEANUT BUTTER COOKIES, PAGE 178

sweet things

I confess that my true passion is baking and making
sweet puddings and desserts. Soon after my daughter
was diagnosed, I began experimenting with some
existing recipes and going through cookbooks in
search of naturally gluten-free cakes and puddings.
In this chapter you will find some wonderful recipes.
Many of these have been adapted from my previous
cookbook and I can honestly say no one will ever know
that they are gluten-free. In fact, you will find lots of
'gluten eaters' as my daughter calls anyone who can eat
gluten, asking you for the recipe.

SWEET THINGS

Yummy Tummy Cake SERVES 10–12

Ruthie named this cake. The recipe is based on a Mexican version known as *Torta del Cielo*, which means Heavenly Cake. It has many culinary uses; as a base for a trifle; layered with strawberries, raspberries and cream; or just eat it plain drizzled with a bit of chocolate syrup.

225 g (7½ oz) ground almonds
65 g (2½ oz) gluten-free plain flour
1 tsp gluten-free baking powder
10 eggs, separated

275 g (9 oz) caster sugar
1 tsp vanilla extract
A pinch of salt
Icing sugar, to dust

● Pre-heat the oven to 190°C (375°F) Gas 5.
● Cut a piece of greaseproof paper to fit the bottom of a 25 cm (10 in) tube pan or angel food cake tin. Grease the paper very lightly with a tiny bit of melted butter but do not grease the sides of the pan!
● In a large bowl combine the almonds, flour and baking powder. In a separate bowl, beat the egg yolks, adding the sugar gradually until the mixture is light and leaves a trail on the surface of the mixture. Add the vanilla extract and the dry ingredients (almonds, flour, baking powder).
● In another bowl whisk the egg whites with a pinch of salt until soft peaks form. Put a third of the egg whites into the egg yolk, sugar and flour mixture. Using a large metal spoon, combine until all the whites are fully incorporated. Now add another third of the

egg whites and combine gently. Add the remaining third trying to keep as much air in the mixture as possible. Pour the mixture into the prepared tin and then bake for approximately 50 minutes until a tester inserted in the middle comes out clean.

● Carefully place the cake on a cooling rack and allow to cool for half an hour, then place it upside down and allow to cool completely. Turn right side up when ready to serve. Serve plain or dusted with icing sugar.

Note: The cake may shrink when you take it out of the oven. Leave it to sit for 5 minutes upright, then turn upside down to cool on a wire rack for at least 1 hour.

MEXICAN CAKE

SWEET THINGS

Apple Hazelnut Loaf (MAKES 1 LARGE LOAF)

This is a delicious light loaf cake that is easy to make. The combination of hazelnuts and apples is a classic, but you can of course experiment using walnuts or pecans or any other nuts you may have to hand.

50 g (2 oz) hazelnuts
2 tbsp milk
¼ tsp vinegar
150 g (5 oz) apple (Braeburn, Cox or Granny Smith)
Juice of 1 lemon
1 tbsp grated lemon zest
150 g (5 oz) gluten-free plain flour

½ tsp bicarbonate of soda
1 tsp xanthan gum
1 tsp gluten-free baking powder
½ tsp salt
100 g (4 oz) unsalted butter
250 g (8 oz) caster sugar
2 eggs
75 g (3 oz) dried cranberries

● Pre-heat the oven to 170°C (325°F) Gas 3. Line a 23 x 12 x 7 cm (9¼ x 5½ in) loaf tin with a greaseproof paper liner or grease lightly.
● Place the hazelnuts on a baking sheet and toast in the oven for about 7 minutes until they are fragrant. Leave them to cool for a few minutes and then grind them in a food processor until they are a fine powder.
● Combine the milk and vinegar in a small bowl and set aside. Core the apples and roughly chop, leaving the skin on. Sprinkle with lemon juice to stop them discolouring.

FRUIT AND NUT ♡ ♡

- In a large bowl combine the flour, ground hazelnuts, bicarbonate of soda, xanthan gum, baking powder and salt.
- In a separate bowl cream the butter and sugar until light and fluffy. Add the eggs one by one, beating well after each addition. The mixture should look like mayonnaise. Add the flour mixture alternately with the milk. Fold in the chopped apple, dried cranberries and lemon zest. Do not overmix.
- Pour the mixture into the prepared loaf tin. Bake for 45–50 minutes or until a skewer inserted in the centre comes out clean. Leave to cool for 10 minutes before turning out on to a wire rack. Leave to cool fully before serving.

Note: It's important to use a loaf tin broadly the same size and shape indicated. If you are using a smaller loaf tin, then fill only to two thirds of the way up and decrease the baking time slightly. Use any remaining batter to fill either another tin or make cupcakes. If you overfill the tin, the cake will take much longer to bake and the texture will not be as good.

BECAUSE OF THE LACK OF GLUTEN, YOU MAY FIND THAT THE TEXTURE IS A BIT CRUMBLY, BUT IN MY MIND THAT JUST ADDS TO THE CHARM.

SWEET THINGS

Carrot Cake SERVES 10

This is adapted from my last cookbook, *The Little Red Barn Baking Book*. It is everything a good carrot cake should be: moist, dense and decadent.

100 g (4 oz) gluten-free plain flour
125 g (4½ oz) ground almonds
2 tsp gluten-free baking powder
1 tsp xanthan gum
1½ tsp bicarbonate of soda
1 tsp ground cinnamon
1 tsp salt
4 eggs
345 g (11½ oz) sugar
275 ml (9 fl oz) sunflower oil

300 g (10 oz) grated carrots
(about 3 large carrots)

FOR THE FROSTING
225 g (7½ oz) soft cream cheese
225 g (7½ oz) unsalted butter
200–300 g (7–10 oz) icing sugar, sifted
2 tsp vanilla extract

● Pre-heat the oven to 180°C (350°F) Gas 4. Butter and flour two 23 cm (9 in) round, 5 cm (2 in) deep cake tins. Chill in the fridge.
● Sift the flour, ground almonds, baking powder, bicarbonate of soda, cinnamon and salt into a large bowl. In a separate bowl using an electric mixer beat the eggs at high speed. Add the sugar and continue beating until pale and fluffy for about 5 minutes. Add the sunflower oil in a steady stream and continue beating until the mixture holds a ribbon-like trail on the surface. Fold in the grated carrots using a metal spoon and then the flour.
● Pour the mixture into the prepared tins and bake for 30–40 minutes or until a wooden skewer inserted into the centre comes

MOIST CAKE

out clean. Leave to cool in the tins for 10–15 minutes before turning out on to a wire rack. Allow to cool completely before icing with soft cheese frosting.

To make the frosting
● Beat the cream cheese and butter together using an electric mixer. Add the sugar in thirds, mixing well after each addition. Test for desired level of sweetness and add the vanilla extract. Chill for 1 hour before using.

YOU NEED TO USE AN ELECTRIC MIXER FOR THIS CAKE TO GET A GOOD RESULT.

SWEET THINGS

Marina's Upside Down Fruit Cake `SERVES 6`

Marina, our Russian neighbour, brought me a piece of this cake one day. It was so delicious I asked her for the recipe. When she wrote it down for me, I couldn't quite believe that was all there was to it. Here is the gluten-free version, which is equally delicious.

3 eggs
250 g (8 oz) caster sugar
150 g (5 oz) gluten-free plain flour
150 g (5 oz) ground almonds

FOR THE TOPPING
1 apple, peeled, cored and chopped

40 g (1½ oz) raisins
75g (3 oz) dried ready-to-eat apricots, chopped
75 g (3 oz) dried plums, chopped
50 g (2 oz) pecans, roughly chopped
15 g (½ oz) caster sugar
15 g (½ oz) demerara sugar
15 g (½ oz) butter, melted

● Pre-heat the oven to 190°C (375°F) Gas 5. Line a loaf tin measuring 23 x 13 cm (9 x 5 in) with a greaseproof paper liner. Alternatively, grease the base of the tin well with a little melted butter and cut a piece of greaseproof paper to fit at the base of the tin.
● In a medium bowl beat the eggs with an electric whisk. Gradually add the sugar until the mixture is pale and mousse-like. Gently fold in the flour and ground almonds.

EAT WARM FROM THE OVEN ♡ ♡

● In another bowl combine the chopped apple, raisins, apricots, plums and pecans. Sprinkle the fruit with the sugars and mix. Stir in the melted butter.

● Spread the fruit mixture on the bottom of the tin in an even layer. Pour the egg and sugar mixture on top and spread evenly to cover the fruit. The mixture may come up almost to the top of the tin. Leave at least 1 cm (3/8 in) at the top of tin so the cake has some room to expand whilst baking. Bake 45–55 minutes until a tester inserted into the middle of the cake comes out clean. Leave to cool for 10 minutes on a wire rack. Tip the tin upside down and peel off the greaseproof paper. Leave to cool completely before serving.

Variation: You can use any combination of dried fruit or nuts to make this cake. Try substituting fresh pear, walnuts, prunes and dates for an equally delicious cake.

THIS CAKE IS IRRESISTIBLE JUST WARM OUT OF THE OVEN, BUT IT ALSO KEEPS FOR A FEW DAYS.

IRRESISTIBLE!

SWEET THINGS

Marble Cake `SERVES 6`

This moist and dense cake is a joy to look at and very tasty too. My guess is that it will keep quite well for a few days, but it never lasts more than a day in our house. It's also a great picnic cake.

125 g (4½ oz) gluten-free plain flour
125 g (4½ oz) ground almonds
1 tbsp gluten-free baking powder
½ tsp salt
1 tsp xanthan gum
50 g (2 oz) plain chocolate

150 g (5 oz) unsalted butter
200 g (7 oz) caster sugar
3 eggs, separated
1 tsp vanilla extract
100 ml (3½ fl oz) milk
50 ml (2 fl oz) soured cream

● Pre-heat the oven to 190°C (375°F) Gas 5. Butter and flour a 23 x 13 x 5 cm (9 x 5 x 2 in) deep loaf tin, or line with a greaseproof paper liner.
● Combine the flour, ground almonds, baking powder, salt and xanthan gum in a bowl. Set aside. Melt the chocolate in a double boiler or bowl set over a pan of simmering water. Stir until smooth.
● In a separate bowl cream the butter with the sugar until pale and lemon-coloured. Add the egg yolks one at a time, beating well after each addition. Add the vanilla extract and soured cream. Finally, add the milk alternately with the dry ingredients.
● In a separate bowl whisk the egg whites until they form soft peaks. Add one third of the whites to the cake mixture and mix through gently until incorporated. Now add the remaining egg

whites and gently fold in using the minimum amount of strokes. Transfer half of this mixture into another bowl and add the melted chocolate. Fold through to incorporate evenly.

● Drop alternate spoonfuls of the vanilla and chocolate mixture into the prepared tin. Run a sharp knife through the mixture and swirl gently to blend slightly. Bake for about 45 minutes or until a wooden skewer inserted in the centre comes out clean. Leave to cool on a wire rack before turning out. Allow to cool completely before serving.

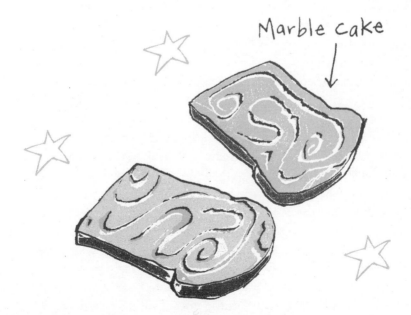

Marble cake

SWEET THINGS

Chocolate and Vanilla Swirly Puddings `SERVES 4`

In America, a pudding is a type of custard and this is what these are. It's the type of dessert you'll find in a classic American diner – a velvety smooth vanilla and chocolate custard which is simple and yet sooooo gorgeous.

450 ml (¾ pint) whole milk
3 egg yolks
65 g (2½ oz) caster sugar
1 tbsp cornflour
1 tsp vanilla extract
40 g (1½ oz) unsalted butter

50 g (2 oz) plain chocolate, finely chopped

TO SERVE
Whipped cream
Chocolate sprinkles

● In a saucepan heat the milk until it just about comes to the boil. In a medium bowl whisk the egg yolks, sugar and cornflour. Add the warm milk to the egg yolk mixture. Pour the yolk and milk mixture through a fine sieve and then pour into a clean saucepan.
● Continue to stir the mixture over a low heat until it starts to thicken. This can take up to 15 minutes. Do not allow it to boil as this will curdle the custard and you will end up with scrambled eggs. The custard is ready when you draw a spoon through it and you can see the bottom of the pan.
● Remove from the heat and stir in the vanilla extract and the butter. Pour half of the custard into a bowl. Add the chopped

SIMPLE AND GORGEOUS

chocolate to the remaining custard in the saucepan. Stir through until the chocolate has melted completely.

● Now spoon the mixture into glasses, alternating spoonfuls of chocolate and vanilla custard. Using the tip of a sharp knife, swirl through the custard. Allow to cool and then place in the fridge for a few hours before serving.

● For the full-on diner effect, serve with fresh whipped cream and chocolate sprinkles.

Note: Do not be tempted to double the recipe as it may not work out. It will take a long time for you to achieve a custard-like consistency and it is also likely to go horribly wrong. If you need a bigger quantity than this, it's best to make two separate batches.

PUDDING TIME ♡ ♡

SWEET THINGS

FOR AN APPLE AND BLACKBERRY CRUMBLE, USE 1 PUNNET OF BLACKBERRIES AND 3 MEDIUM APPLES, PEELED, CORED AND CUT INTO CHUNKS.

Apple and Rhubarb Crumble SERVES 4–6

This is an easy crumble, which you can vary according to the seasons. Try cherries and peaches in the summer or pear and plums in the winter.

3–4 medium apples
6–8 rhubarb stalks
Demerara sugar
(a liberal sprinkling)

FOR THE CRUMBLE
50 g (2 oz) gluten-free plain flour

50 g (2 oz) polenta
50 g (2 oz) caster sugar
65 g (2½ oz) ground almonds
75 g (3 oz) chopped nuts, toasted
(pecans, almonds, hazelnuts)
100 g (4 oz) cold unsalted
butter, diced

- Pre-heat the oven to 180°C (350°F) Gas 4.
- Peel, core and slice the apples into chunks. Peel the rhubarb, removing the stringy bits and cut into 1.5 cm (½ in) chunks. Place the fruit in an ovenproof dish and sprinkle liberally with demerara sugar. Set aside for a few minutes.
- To make the crumble, combine the flour, polenta, sugar, ground almonds and chopped nuts in the bowl of a food processor. Add the chunks of butter and whiz the mixture until it resembles coarse breadcrumbs. Sprinkle the crumble over the fruit.
- Bake for 40–45 minutes until the fruit is tender and the top is golden. Leave to cool for a few minutes before serving with ice cream, double cream or custard.

LUXURIOUS!

Fruity Mousse SERVES 6

A very quick and easy mousse that doesn't require gelatine.
If your children are old enough, serve this in glass goblets –
it makes an impressive pudding.

250 ml (8 fl oz) double cream
200 ml (7 fl oz) Greek yoghurt
Summer Fruits Sauce (page 190)

● Put the cream in a bowl and whisk until very soft peaks form.
Fold in the yoghurt. Add about half of the fruit sauce and mix
through gently. You should have a luxurious soft cream.
● Pour the remainder of the fruit sauce into 6 ramekins or goblets.
Spoon the mousse on top of the sauce. Put in the fridge and allow
to set for a few hours before serving.

QUICK AND EASY
♡ ♡

SWEET THINGS

Snickerdoodles (MAKES ABOUT 30 COOKIES)

This is a classic American cookie with a great name. You can make these from start to finish in less than half an hour.

375 g (12 oz) gluten-free plain flour
½ tsp salt
¼ tsp bicarbonate of soda
1 tsp cream of tartar
1 tsp xanthan gum
225 g (7½ oz) butter
300 g (10 oz) caster sugar
1½ tsp vanilla extract

2 eggs
50 ml (2 fl oz) milk

FOR THE TOPPING
1 tsp caster sugar
1 tbsp demerara sugar
1 tsp ground cinnamon

● Pre-heat the oven to 190°C (375°F) Gas 5. Lightly grease two baking sheets.

● Combine the flour, salt, bicarbonate of soda, cream of tartar and xanthan gum in a bowl. In a separate bowl cream the butter and sugar until pale and fluffy. Add the vanilla extract, eggs and milk and combine thoroughly. Fold in the dry ingredients and combine to make a soft dough.

● Combine the ingredients for the topping in a small bowl. Using a teaspoon, drop a spoonful of cookie dough into the topping mix and roll in the topping. Gently lift out and place on the prepared baking sheets. Continue until all the cookie dough has been used up.

● Bake the cookies for 12–15 minutes until puffed and golden. Leave to cool on the baking sheet for a few minutes before transferring on to a wire rack. Serve straight away.

(MAKES 24
COOKIES)

Chocolate Truffle Cookies

Easy to make and pretty to look at, these cookies have the wow factor, especially if you serve them straight out of the oven.

65 g (2½ oz) gluten-free
plain flour
100 g (4 oz) caster sugar
40 g (1½ oz) cocoa powder
½ tsp gluten-free baking powder
¼ tsp salt

¼ tsp xanthan gum
25 g (1 oz) unsalted butter,
diced
1 egg
1 tbsp milk
Icing sugar

● Sift the flour, sugar, cocoa, baking powder, salt and xanthan gum into a large bowl. Rub in the butter using your fingers, then add the egg and milk. Chill the dough in the freezer for about 20 minutes until it's firm enough to handle.

● Pre-heat the oven to 200°C (400°F) Gas 6, and lightly grease two baking sheets.

● Take a scoop of dough with a teaspoon and roll into a ball. Roll the ball in icing sugar, then place on the prepared baking sheet, leaving room for spreading. Continue until all the dough is used up. Bake for 8–10 minutes or until just set. Leave to cool before transferring on to a wire rack. These are best eaten within minutes of coming out of the oven, but they will keep for a day or two in an airtight container.

YOU CAN ALSO MAKE THE DOUGH AHEAD OF TIME AND STORE IT IN THE FREEZER. SHAPE INTO BALLS, ROLL IN ICING SUGAR AND BAKE FROM FROZEN.

SWEET THINGS

Peanut Butter Cookies

I spotted this recipe in a magazine many years ago. I was intrigued by the lack of flour and the simplicity of ingredients. These cookies are light, crunchy and flavourful. You can make a batch in a matter of minutes.

175 g (6 oz) caster sugar
200 g (7 oz) peanut butter
(smooth or crunchy)

I egg
I tsp bicarbonate of soda

● Pre-heat the oven to 180°C (350°F) Gas 4. Line a baking sheet with greaseproof paper.
● Combine the sugar and peanut butter. Add the egg and baking soda. Roll the mixture into balls and place on the prepared baking sheet. Flatten the balls with the tines of a fork.
● Bake in the oven 10–15 minutes until golden. Eat straight away or store in an airtight container for about 1 week.

YOU WILL NEED SOME SPECIAL EQUIPMENT FOR THIS RECIPE: AN ELECTRIC MIXER AND A PLASTIC BAG OR PIPING BAG WITH A STRAIGHT NOZZLE

Lady Fingers

These plain biscuits are quick to make and keep well in an airtight tin. In France they are known as *Langue de Chat* and in Latin America as *Lenguas de Gato!* A good biscuit for the gluten-free baby in your life.

3 eggs, separated
100 g (4 oz) caster sugar, plus 1 tbsp
1 tsp vanilla extract

A pinch of salt
100 g (4 oz) gluten-free plain flour, sifted
Icing sugar

● Pre-heat the oven to 150°C (300°F) Gas 2. Line two baking sheets with greaseproof paper or silicone baking liners. Prepare a piping bag or a clean medium-sized plastic bag.
● In a small bowl measure out the flour and set aside.
● In a medium bowl combine the egg yolks and 100 g (4 oz) of sugar and beat until pale and ribbony. Add the vanilla and the flour.
● In another bowl beat the egg whites with the salt until soft peaks form. Add the remaining tablespoon of sugar and continue beating for another minute.
● Now add a third of the egg whites to the egg yolk and sugar mixture and fold in gently with a large metal spoon. Add the remaining egg whites in the same way.
● Spoon the mixture into the plastic bag or piping bag. Snip off a very small corner of the plastic bag and quickly pipe into fingers leaving some room for them to expand. Bake for 20–30 minutes until crisp. Leave to cool for a few minutes and then transfer to a wire rack.

SWEET THINGS

Grandma Eve's Mandelbrot (MAKES ABOUT 40 BISCOTTI)

Mandelbrot is a Jewish biscotti. Grandma Eve was famous for her Mandelbrot and I'm so pleased that I've managed to make them gluten-free. Light, crunchy and crumbly, these always get top marks.

I tsp ground cinnamon
3–4 tsp demerara sugar
3 eggs
175 g (6 oz) caster sugar
250 ml (8 fl oz) sunflower oil
¼ tsp almond essence
A pinch of salt

I tbsp gluten-free baking powder
I tsp bicarbonate of soda
250 g (8 oz) gluten-free plain flour
250 g (8 oz) ground almonds
100 g (4 oz) roasted almonds, chopped

● Pre-heat the oven to 180°C (350°F) Gas 4.
● Line a large baking sheet with greaseproof paper. In a small bowl combine the cinnamon and demerara sugar.
● In a large mixing bowl combine the eggs and sugar. Beat with an electric mixer until pale and light. Continue beating the eggs and sugar while adding the oil in a steady stream. The mixture should be thick and mousse-like. Add the almond essence.
● In a separate bowl combine the salt, baking powder, baking soda, flour and ground almonds. Mix gently. Fold the dry ingredients into the egg mixture. It will be a thick sticky batter. Pour the batter on to the baking sheet, spreading it out evenly with

a spatula. Sprinkle the top with the sugar and cinnamon mixture.
● Bake for 25–30 minutes until just golden. Leave to cool for a few
minutes then slice into 4 cm (1½ in) fingers. Place these on baking
sheets and lower the oven temperature to 150°C (300°F) Gas 2.
Bake for a further 15–20 minutes until light and crunchy. Leave to
cool and store in an airtight tin.

Brownies (MAKES 16–20 BROWNIES)

I won't be modest, these brownies are the best! They are
moist, chocolatey and chewy and no one will ever guess that
something gluten-free can taste this fantastic. The good news
is they are really easy to make – just follow the tips at the
bottom of the recipe.

100 g (4 oz) good quality plain
chocolate (minimum 70% cocoa
solids)
100 g (4 oz) unsalted butter
150 g (5 oz) dark soft brown sugar
150 g (5 oz) caster sugar
2 eggs

¼ tsp salt
1 tsp vanilla extract
150 g (5 oz) ground almonds
50 g (2 oz) marshmallows (cut
into small pieces)
100 g (4 oz) toasted pecans
(optional)

Brownies continued

● Pre-heat the oven to 170°C (325°F) Gas 3. Line a 22 cm (8½ in) square tin with a large square of foil. (You can also use a disposable square tin measuring about the same, and just brush lightly with a little sunflower oil.) Make sure the corners are carefully lined. Using a pastry brush, lightly grease the foil with a very small amount of sunflower oil, making sure the corners are well greased.

● Melt the chocolate and butter in a double boiler or a bowl set over a pan of simmering water (you can also use a microwave), taking care the chocolate does not overheat. Stir the mixture. It should look very shiny and glossy. Remove from the heat and add the sugars and stir through allowing the sugar to dissolve a bit. The mixture may look a bit grainy at this stage but this is completely normal.

● Add the eggs, beating well and once again the mixture will be thick and glossy. Add the salt and vanilla and then fold in the ground almonds and finally the chopped marshmallows and toasted pecans, if using. Make sure everything is well incorporated but do not overmix (you do not want lots of air in the mixture). The mixture will be quite thick and reluctant to pour.

● Spread the mixture into the prepared tin to form an even layer. Bake for approximately 20–25 minutes or until it is just set in the middle and the edges are slightly coming away from the pan. A wooden skewer inserted in the middle should come out with just a few moist crumbs on it. If it is totally gooey, place back in the oven to bake for a few more minutes. This will not harm the brownies so check them as often as required.

IF YOU PRESS WITH YOUR FINGER ON THE TOP OF THE BROWNIES, THEY SHOULD BE FIRM, BUT STILL GIVE A LITTLE.

- Once they are done, leave them to cool completely in the tin before cutting them.
- To serve, invert the pan and then very gently peel off the foil. (If you are using a disposable tin, just press the edges of the pan to loosen the brownie a bit, invert the tin and carefully peel the tin away from the base. It should peel away easily). Place the brownies on a board and using a sharp knife, cut into squares and dust with icing sugar.

Note: I like to make these brownies the night before. Leave them in the tin overnight without cutting them. This allows them to firm up a bit. Then cut, dust with icing sugar and serve.

Tips for making great brownies
- Do not overmix the batter. You don't want lots of air in the mixture.
- Always make brownies in a square pan.
- Don't overbake but also don't underbake!

To test if the brownies are ready
Insert a wooden toothpick in the centre. There should be a few moist crumbs when you remove it. The edges should just slightly be pulling away from the pan.

Brownie

SWEET THINGS

Dalia's Luscious Lemon Bars *(MAKES 24–30 BARS)*

Here's a recipe from my baby sister, Dalia. Lemon bars always get rave reviews. They are light, lemony and really, really delicious.

FOR THE BASE
125 g (4½ oz) gluten-free
plain flour
125 g (4½ oz) ground almonds
50 g (2 oz) icing sugar
200 g (7 oz) cold unsalted
butter, diced

FOR THE TOPPING
4 eggs
400 g (13 oz) caster sugar
75 ml (3 fl oz) freshly squeezed
lemon juice (about 2 small lemons)
25 g (1 oz) gluten-free plain flour
½ tsp gluten-free baking powder
Icing sugar, to dust

● Pre-heat the oven to 180°C (350°F) Gas 4.
● To make the base, combine the flour, ground almonds and icing sugar in a large bowl. Rub the butter into the flour mixture using your fingertips to make a soft dough. You can use a food processor to do this but use the pulse button sparingly and be careful not to overmix the dough or it will go greasy.
● Press the dough into the bottom of a 33 x 23 cm (13 x 9 in) cake tin as evenly as possible but try not to overwork the dough. If you use a smaller or larger tin, remember you may need to adjust your baking times accordingly. Bake for 15–20 minutes or until the pastry is lightly golden.

LIGHT, LEMONY AND...

● In the meantime, prepare the topping. Beat the eggs, sugar and lemon juice together in a bowl. Stir in the flour and baking powder.

● When the base is ready, remove from the oven and leave it to cool for a few minutes. Pour the topping over the base. Bake for a further 25 minutes or until the filling is just set. Leave to cool in the pan for several hours before dusting with icing sugar and cutting into bars.

Note: The lemon bars can be kept in the fridge for several days or can be frozen.

REALLY ♡ ♡ DELICIOUS!

Magic Bars (MAKES ABOUT 24–30 BARS)

Another recipe from my sister Dalia that I've adapted to be gluten-free. Chunky, chocolatey, gooey, sweet, creamy and a little bit salty, they are unbelievably good. The best news is they are quick and easy to make.

85 g (3½ oz) unsalted butter
¼ tsp salt (optional)
85 g (3½ oz) gluten-free cornflakes
85 g (3½ oz) pecans
250 g (8 oz) plain chocolate chips

125 g (4½ oz) desiccated coconut
85 g (3½ oz) pecans, roughly chopped
390 g (14 oz) can condensed milk

● Pre-heat the oven to 170°C (325°F) Gas 3.
● Melt the butter and add the salt, if using. In a food processor blend the cornflakes and the pecans until fine. Pour them into a bowl and combine with the melted butter, stirring with a fork. Press the mixture into a 32 x 18 cm (12½ x 7 in) baking tin. Make sure the base of the tin is completely covered.
● In a bowl combine the chocolate chips, the coconut and the chopped pecans. Pour this on top of the base to make an even layer. Then pour the condensed milk evenly over the top. Bake for 25–30 minutes until golden. Allow to cool, then place in the fridge for a few hours (or overnight), before cutting into bars.

Note: The base on these bars is quite crumbly. You can use a tin smaller than suggested which will give you a thicker base. This recipe is unsuitable for young children under the age of 3.

USE FOR PICNICS!

Tropical Rice Crispy Bars *(MAKES ABOUT 20 BARS)*

A tropical take on normal Rice Crispy bars. You can use any dried fruit and feel free to add some roasted nuts and seeds, too.

150 g (5 oz) mixed dried fruit, chopped (apricots, mango, cherries, dates, pears)
150 g (5 oz) gluten-free crispy rice cereal

65 g (2½ oz) unsalted butter
A pinch of salt
200 g (7 oz) marshmallows
1 tsp vanilla extract

- Grease a 22 cm (8½ in) square tin with a little melted butter.
- Measure out the cereal into a large bowl. Using a pair of scissors, chop the dried fruit and add to the cereal. Mix through.
- In a large saucepan melt the butter. Add a pinch of salt, then the marshmallows and melt over low heat. Add the vanilla extract. Pour this onto the cereal and dried fruit and mix through. Pour the mixture into the tin and press down firmly with a wooden spoon press to make sure it is even.
- Refrigerate for a few hours before slicing into squares.

Chocolate Sauce

This simple sauce will add a touch of silky luxury to ice cream, cakes, fresh fruit and marshmallows. You can also use it to make a really spectacular hot chocolate. I've used chocolate chips for speed, but any good chocolate (chopped into equal-sized pieces) will work well.

200 ml (7 fl oz) double cream
140 ml (¼ pint) liquid glucose or corn syrup

200 g (7 oz) plain chocolate chips
A pinch of salt

● In a medium saucepan heat the cream and liquid glucose until it just comes to the boil. Stir gently and then add the chocolate chips. Leave undisturbed, uncovered for 5 minutes, then gently stir to combine. This sauce will remain liquid while still warm, but it will set when cold.

Note: This sauce will keep for about 2 weeks in the fridge. To use from the fridge, just remove the quantity required and put into a small bowl. Heat for a few seconds in a microwave or over a bain-marie until runny.

DRIZZLE AWAY!

Toffee Sauce

This is a lovely, sticky sauce to drizzle over ice cream or fresh fruit kebabs!

75 g (3 oz) caster sugar
75 g (3 oz) light brown sugar
1½ tsp liquid glucose or corn syrup

60 ml (2½ fl oz) water
100 ml (3½ fl oz) double cream
1½ tsp vanilla extract
A pinch of salt

- In a medium saucepan combine the sugars, glucose and water. Gently swish the saucepan to combine the ingredients. Cook over a medium heat, swishing the pan gently until the sugar is dissolved.
- Turn up the heat to high and allow the sauce to boil vigorously for 6–8 minutes. Do not stir the sauce, but gently swish the pan. The sauce will turn a caramel colour. Turn off the heat and pour in the double cream, vanilla and salt. The sauce will bubble up so be careful you don't get splashed. Swish the pan gently to combine. Allow to cool for a few minutes before decanting the sauce to a jug or bowl. Serve warm.
- The sauce will set when cold. To reheat, warm through for a few seconds in a microwave or bain-marie.
- This sauce will keep for 2–3 days in the fridge.

Note: Do not allow children near this sauce when you are making it as hot sugar can cause serious burns.

Summer Fruit Sauce

You can make this sauce with fresh or frozen fruit, so you can have Summer Fruit Sauce all year long. It's a great sauce to have in the fridge on standby. Use it drizzled on ice cream or stirred into Greek yoghurt, or as a little fruity number to give extra pizazz to a chocolate roulade.

350 g (11½ oz) frozen or fresh summer fruit (raspberries, blackberries, red and black currants, mulberries)

25 g (1 oz) caster sugar
Icing sugar

● Put the fruit and sugar in a medium saucepan. Add a few tablespoons of water and gently swish the pan around to dissolve the sugar. Simmer over a medium heat until the fruit is just soft, 5–8 minutes for frozen fruit and a little less for fresh fruit. Let the sauce come to the boil and boil for a minute or so. Taste and add a little icing sugar if you want the sauce a bit sweeter. Leave to cool.
● You can serve the sauce as is, or you can put it through a fine sieve to make a luxurious coulis. Taste again for sweetness. If the coulis appears too runny, you can bring the sauce back up to the boil and cook for a few more minutes until it has reduced to the right consistency. Leave to cool before serving.
● This sauce will keep in the fridge for about 1 week.

LEMONY FRESH ☆

Lemon Curd

This will keep for weeks in the fridge and is incredibly versatile. Use it to make lemon curd ice cream or stir it into Greek yoghurt and serve with biscotti.

6 egg yolks
165 g (5½ oz) caster sugar

100 ml (3½ fl oz) freshly squeezed lemon juice (about 2 lemons)
75 g (3 oz) butter

● Strain the egg yolks into a bowl. Add the sugar and lemon juice and mix well. Pour this into a medium saucepan and cook over a medium-low heat, stirring continuously until the mixture thickens and coats the back of a spoon. The amount of cooking time will depend on the type of saucepan used, so allow anywhere from 5–15 minutes. Do not allow the mixture to boil or it will be ruined.

● When it is thick enough, remove from the heat and whisk in the butter, a little at a time. Leave to cool before storing in a clean sterilised jar or a bowl. If you are planning to keep this for a while, it's best to keep it in a sterilised jar.

Note: If you end up with a grainy texture you can rescue the curd by putting it through a sieve. Let the curd work its way gently through the sieve and discard any solids left behind.

Dips ↓ here

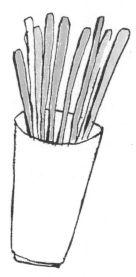

Gingerbread

party food

Everyone loves a good party, but being gluten-free at a party is no picnic. The reality is that most party menus rarely include a single item that is gluten-free. Yet it really is not difficult to make your party 100 per cent gluten-free. In this chapter you will find some recipes for special occasions. Most of these are very straightforward but they may require a little bit extra preparation time and attention. I hope these recipes will help dispel the myth about gluten-free food being boring or weird. There are lots of wonderful things to eat in our gluten-free world. We just need to spread the word.

Four Layer Latin Dip

This is a truly terrific dip. I was given the recipe by Lucy Bland, when I was in charge of editing a Guatemalan newsletter. It's unusual and incredibly simple.

200 g (7 oz) gluten-free refried beans
2 ripe avocados, peeled and stoned
Freshly squeezed juice of 1 lime

1 jar gluten-free taco sauce (mild or hot)
200 ml (7 fl oz) crème fraîche
Tabasco sauce (optional)
Tortilla chips, to serve

● Select a deep container or bowl suitable for serving at the table. Glass will show off the layers best, but if there are lots of young children about, plastic may be a better option. The order of the layers is not critical so this is just a suggestion.

● Start with placing the refried beans at the bottom of the dish. On a large plate mash up the avocado with a fork and add a generous amount of lime juice, some salt and Tabasco, if using. Place this on top of the refried beans. Next, add the taco sauce layer. Finally, add a layer of crème fraîche layer. The dip will sit in the fridge for a few hours if you want to make it in advance. Serve with tortilla chips.

Note: Old el Paso and Discovery refried beans and taco sauce are currently gluten-free, but always check the label as sometimes recipes change.

FOR YOUNG CHILDREN YOU MAY WANT TO KEEP THE SEASONING QUITE MILD. FOR OLDER KIDS, YOU CAN UP THE HEAT A BIT.

QUICK DIPS ♡ ♡

Soft Cheese Herb Dip

There are no precise measurements here, as this is something I make with whatever is in the fridge. It's a great dip to serve with roasted baby potatoes, fish fingers and chicken nuggets.

150 g (5 oz) soft cream cheese
150 ml (¼ pint) soured cream
½ garlic clove
Freshly squeezed juice of ½ lime

10–15 fresh basil leaves
10–15 fresh mint leaves
Chives
Salt

● On a large plate combine the soft cheese and soured cream. Mash thoroughly until you have a smooth creamy consistency. Add some salt. Crush the garlic in a garlic press and mix through, along with the lime juice. Taste and season again if necessary.
● Finely shred the mint and basil leaves. Put the mixture in a bowl and add the herbs and some snipped chives. Mix and serve.

Note: This dip doesn't like hanging around, so make it at the last minute.

DIPS
↓ here

IF YOU HAVE FRESH HERBS FROM THE GARDEN THEN YOU ARE OFF TO A GOOD START.

Guacamole Dip SERVES 6–8

This dip gets huge raves at parties. It's incredibly simple and very effective. Be sure to buy your avocados a few days in advance so that they are perfectly ripe.

2 medium ripe avocados, peeled and stoned
Freshly squeezed juice of 1 lime

Tabasco sauce (optional)
Crème fraîche
Salt

● Mash the avocado on a large plate until it's smooth. Add the lime juice and salt to taste – it should be quite tangy. Add a few drops of Tabasco if you are using it, and mix through. Put the mixture in a bowl and add a few large dollops of crème fraîche and mix together. You are looking for a nice dip consistency. Taste and adjust the seasoning if required.
● The dip will sit happily in the fridge for a few hours.

Avocados

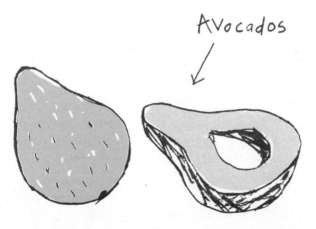

PARTY SNACKS!!

Prairie Mix *SERVES 8*

This is a good snack mix to serve at parties. If you are making this for adults and teenage children you can add some additional chilli heat. Once toasted it keeps well in a sealed jar or tin.

75 g (3 oz) gluten-free cornflakes
75g (3 oz) gluten-free pretzels
100 g (4 oz) peanuts and/or
hazelnuts
150 g (5 oz) almonds and/or
cashews
50 g (2 oz) rice cakes, broken
into large chunks

25 g (1 oz) unsalted butter
1 tbsp gluten-free soy sauce or
Tamari sauce
2 tsp gluten-free curry powder
2 tsp sugar
½ tsp cayenne pepper (optional)
¼ tsp salt

● Pre-heat the oven to 180°C (350°F) Gas 4.
● In a large bowl combine all the dry ingredients and mix together. Melt the butter in the microwave in a small bowl or in a saucepan over a low heat. Add the remaining ingredients to the butter and mix. Pour this liquid on to the dry ingredients and mix together to make sure everything is well coated.
● Pour the mixture on to 2 baking sheets. Put in the oven and bake for 30–40 minutes, stirring every 15–20 minutes. Leave to cool before serving.

Note: This recipe is not suitable for young children under the age of 3.

Lovely Little Cupcakes with Buttercream Icing (Makes 24 mini cupcakes or 12 standard cupcakes)

This is a quick recipe that makes delicious, moist and buttery cupcakes. These cupcakes freeze well and you can even ice them and have them ready to go, for any last-minute parties. This is also a good recipe to make with your children.

100 g (4 oz) gluten-free plain flour
50 g (2 oz) ground almonds
1½ tsp gluten-free baking powder
1½ tsp xanthan gum
½ tsp salt
150 g (5 oz) unsalted butter
175 g (6 oz) caster sugar
3 eggs
1 tsp vanilla extract
1 tbsp milk

FOR THE BUTTERCREAM ICING
200 g (7 oz) icing sugar
50 g (2 oz) unsalted butter
A pinch of salt
3 tbsp milk
1 tsp vanilla extract

● Pre-heat the oven to 180°C (350°F) Gas 4. Line a 12-hole cupcake tin with paper cases, or two 12-hole cupcake tins with mini cupcake cases.
● In a bowl combine the flour, almonds, baking powder, xanthan gum and salt. In a separate bowl cream the butter and sugar until pale and fluffy. Add the eggs one at a time, beating after each addition. The batter should resemble a thick mayonnaise. Add the vanilla extract. Add the flour mixture, mixing gently with a large

DELICIOUS ♡ ♡
AND MOIST

metal spoon. Do not overmix. Add the milk. Spoon the mixture into the lined cupcake tins.

● Bake for about 10 minutes for mini cupcakes or about 15 minutes for standard cupcakes. Leave to cool on a wire rack, while you prepare the icing.

To make icing

● Sift the icing sugar into a large bowl, removing any lumps.

● Cream the butter and sugar. Add the salt and vanilla, and then the milk. Beat until you reach a soft spreading consistency. Spread generously over each cupcake and enjoy!

cupcakes

THE KEY TO GOOD BUTTERCREAM *ICING IS* STARTING WITH GOOD UNSALTED BUTTER.

ONCE YOU'VE MASTERED THIS YOU CAN THEN EXPERIMENT BY ADDING DIFFERENT FLAVOURS LIKE CHOCOLATE, LEMON AND MAPLE SYRUP.

PARTY FOOD

Breadsticks (MAKES ABOUT 30 BREADSTICKS)

These breadsticks are addictive and they are at their absolute best hot out of the oven. Serve with dips, chilli con carne, soup or just munch on their own.

1 x recipe for Quick Pizza (page 66)
Gluten-free plain flour

Salt (optional)
Sesame seeds (optional)

- Pre-heat the oven to 180°C (350°F) Gas 4.
- Prepare the dough as per the recipe for Quick Pizza on page 66. Cut the dough into quarters and sprinkle flour on a smooth work surface. Take a quarter of the dough and roll it out to about 1 cm (3/8 in) thickness. Using a very sharp knife, cut the dough into strips. Gently roll the strips to make a thin breadstick and place on a baking sheet. Continue this process until all the dough has been used.
- Using a pastry brush, lightly brush the sticks with water. Sprinkle with sea salt and/or sesame seeds. It is not essential to do this step so if you just want plain breadsticks, put straight into the oven. Bake 10–15 minutes until crisp.
- If you prefer chewier breadsticks, then roll them out a little bit thicker and bake a little less.

Note: You can keep breadsticks in an airtight tin for a few days although you will need to refresh them in the oven before serving. To do this, pre-heat your oven, put the breadsticks on a baking sheet and bake for 5–10 minutes until crispy.

SPECTACULAR!

Brenda's Lemon Meringue Ice Cream Cake SERVES 8–10

My friend Brenda gave me this recipe many years ago and it's one I really treasure. It makes a spectacular birthday cake. Naturally gluten-free, light, lemony and absolutely delicious.

FOR THE MERINGUE
4 egg whites at room temperature
A pinch of salt
250 g (8 oz) caster sugar
Zest of 1 lemon

FOR THE LEMON CURD ICE CREAM
300 ml (½ pint) single cream

100 g (4 oz) caster sugar
300 ml (½ pint) Greek yoghurt
275 ml (9 fl oz) double cream, whipped
1 jar good quality lemon curd (or 1 quantity Lemon Curd recipe, page 191)
Icing sugar, to serve

To make the meringue

● Pre-heat the oven to 140°C (275°F) Gas 1. Line two baking sheets with a sheet of baking parchment. Trace around the base of a 23 cm (9 in) springform cake tin on to each sheet of baking parchment. This will leave you with two circles, one on each baking sheet.

● In a large bowl whisk the egg whites and salt with an electric mixer until stiff. Gradually add the sugar, bit by bit, until the whites are glossy and stiff. Add the lemon zest and mix through. Carefully spread the meringue on to the prepared baking sheets,

Brenda's Lemon Meringue
Ice Cream Cake continued

using the traced circles as a guide. Divide the mixture evenly to make two meringue disks. Bake the meringue for about 1 hour. It is ready when it comes away from the paper easily. Cool on a wire rack.

To make the ice cream with an ice cream maker

● Warm the cream and sugar in a saucepan over low heat until the sugar has dissolved. Leave to cool for a few minutes. Add the yoghurt and whisk. Pour the mixture into your ice cream maker, and proceed as per your machine instructions.

● To the ready-made ice cream, fold in the whipped double cream and the lemon curd. Place the mixture in a 23 cm (9 in) springform tin, cover with clingfilm and then put in the freezer to firm up overnight. Allow a minimum of 6 hours.

To make the ice cream with a food processor

● Warm the cream and sugar in a saucepan over low heat until the sugar has dissolved. Leave to cool for a few minutes. Add the yoghurt and whisk. Place the cream, sugar and yoghurt mixture in a metal tin and freeze for a few hours until just firm. When the mixture is firm, put it in the bowl of a food processor and whiz until smooth. Pour out into a large bowl and quickly fold in the whipped double cream and lemon curd. Put the mixture in a 23 cm (9 in) springform tin, cover with clingfilm and then put in the freezer to firm up overnight. Allow a minimum of 6 hours.

LIGHT AND LEMONY

To assemble the cake

● Place one meringue disc on to a large piece of foil. Remove the ice cream from the springform tin and place on top of the meringue. Sandwich with the other meringue and then wrap up gently in the foil. Place the parcel in the freezer and leave to set for at least 6 hours or overnight. It will keep quite happily for about 1 month.

To serve

Remove from the freezer a good 15 minutes before serving. Unwrap carefully and place on a serving dish. Dust with icing sugar.

Variation: You can use this idea to make any number of ice cream cakes. Layers of strawberry, vanilla and chocolate ice cream will look really festive and will go down well with younger children. You could also try combining ready–made vanilla ice cream with Lemon Curd (see p191 or buy one ready–made) for a quicker version of Lemon Curd Ice Cream.

YOU WILL NEED TO START THIS DESSERT A FEW DAYS IN ADVANCE, BUT THIS IS ACTUALLY TO YOUR ADVANTAGE.

THE FULLY ASSEMBLED CAKE CAN SIT IN THE FREEZER FOR UP TO 1 MONTH, WITHOUT ANY PROBLEM.

ON THE DAY OF THE PARTY, REMOVE IT FROM THE FREEZER 15 MINUTES BEFORE SERVING.

Chocolate Chip Cake (MAKES 1 LARGE CAKE SERVES 12–15)

The inspiration for this recipe comes from Hesh's Bakery in Philadelphia. This cake is golden and dense with zillions of chocolate chips.

200 g (7 oz) gluten-free plain flour
150 g (5 oz) ground almonds
½ tsp salt
¼ tsp bicarbonate of soda
225 g (7½ oz) unsalted butter
625 g (1¼ lb) caster sugar

6 eggs
1 tsp vanilla extract
225 ml (7½ fl oz) crème fraîche or soured cream
175 g (6 oz) good quality chocolate, roughly chopped

● Pre-heat the oven to 170°C (325°F) Gas 3. Lightly grease and flour a large 25 cm (9¾ in) cake tin. Chill in the fridge.
● Sift the flour, ground almonds, salt and bicarbonate of soda into a large bowl. In a separate bowl cream the butter with the sugar until pale and fluffy. Add the eggs one by one, beating well after each addition. The mixture should have the consistency of mayonnaise. Add the vanilla extract and the crème fraîche. Fold in the dry ingredients and the chocolate chunks. Don't overmix.
● Pour the mixture into the prepared tin. Bake for 1 hour 20 minutes or until a wooden skewer inserted in the centre of the cake comes out clean. Leave to cool in the tin for 30 minutes before turning out onto a wire rack. Allow to cool completely before decorating with Buttercream icing (page 198).

Note: This cake freezes well. Freeze uniced.

DELECTABLE!!

IF YOU CAN, MAKE THIS A DAY IN ADVANCE, AS THE FLAVOUR AND TEXTURE IMPROVE IF LEFT TO STAND FOR A DAY OR SO.

PARTY FOOD

Chocolate Roulade *SERVES 6–8*

Here's a great recipe from Leith's, which is naturally gluten-free. Do not worry if, as you start to roll up the roulade, huge cracks appear. Any wayward bits or cracks are easily disguised with a good sprinkling of icing sugar.

5 eggs, separated
150 g (5 oz) caster sugar
225 g (7½ oz) plain chocolate, chopped
75 ml (3 fl oz) water
1 tsp instant coffee

FOR THE FILLING
275 ml (9 fl oz) double cream
Fresh raspberries or strawberries

● Pre-heat the oven to 200°C (400°F) Gas 6. Prepare a large baking sheet with a large sheet of baking parchment (not greaseproof paper as this will stick) that slightly overhangs the corners of the baking sheet.
● Beat the egg yolks with the sugar until pale and mousse-like.
● Put the chocolate, water and coffee into a heatproof bowl. Place this over a pan of simmering water, but make sure the bottom of the bowl is not in contact with the water. Gently melt the chocolate, stirring occasionally. When melted, fold the chocolate into the egg yolk and sugar mixture.
● In a separate bowl whisk the egg whites until they form stiff peaks. Using a large metal spoon, gently fold a third of the egg whites into the chocolate to loosen the mixture. Add the remaining egg whites, folding carefully to retain as much air in the mixture as

possible. Spread the batter evenly into the prepared baking sheet.

● Bake for 10–12 minutes until the top is just firm to the touch. Slide the parchment paper out of the baking sheet and place the roulade on a wire rack and cover with a tea towel. Leave to cool completely. You can leave it overnight.

● To prepare the filling, whip the cream until you reach very soft peaks. It's really important not to over beat the cream because the texture will be a bit chalky. Stop beating the cream just short of soft peaks. The cream will stiffen up a bit more while it stands. Spread the cream evenly on to the roulade and dot with raspberries. Carefully roll up using the parchment paper to help. Transfer the roulade on to a serving plate. Dust with icing sugar before serving, disguising any cracks that may have appeared.

Variation: You can also bake this recipe as cupcakes. Line cupcake tins with 24 paper liners. Fill until just over halfway. Bake for 7–10 minutes until just firm. Ice with Buttercream Icing (page 198) or just put a dollop of whipped cream on top of each cupcake and top with sprinkles.

PARTY FOOD

Chocolate Fudge (MAKES 25–30 PIECES)

This fudge is smooth, nutty and gorgeous. I like this recipe because you don't need a sugar thermometer or a degree in chemistry. It's very straightforward and the results are scrumptious.

100 g (4 oz) nuts (hazelnuts work very well) – see note
225 g (7½ oz) caster sugar
65 g (2½ oz) unsalted butter
150 ml (¼ pint) evaporated milk

¼ tsp salt
350 g (11½ oz) good quality plain chocolate, chopped
1 tsp vanilla extract
200 g (7 oz) marshmallows

● Pre-heat the oven to 180°C (350°F) Gas 4. Toast the nuts in the oven for about 10 minutes until just golden. Leave to cool and then chop roughly. Lightly grease a tin measuring approximately 22 cm (8½ in) with a little sunflower oil.
● In a medium saucepan combine the sugar, butter, evaporated milk and salt. Boil for 4 minutes and then remove from the heat. Add the chopped chocolate, vanilla and the marshmallows. Stir until blended, then add the nuts.
● Pour the mixture into the prepared tin and leave to cool. Refrigerate for at least 2 hours. To serve, cut the fudge into small squares.

Note: If you are making this for young children, please omit the nuts and replace with sultanas or raisins.

ALMOST VIRTUOUS!

Crazy Crunchy Cakes

(MAKES ABOUT 48 MINI MUFFIN SIZE CAKES)

I like to think these little cakes are fairly healthy. The addition of sesame seeds and tahini makes them feel quite virtuous and a little bit of plain chocolate never hurt anyone.

75 g (3 oz) plain chocolate, chopped
50 g (2 oz) butter
140 ml liquid glucose or corn syrup

75 g (3 oz) gluten-free Rice Crispies
25 g (1 oz) gluten-free cornflakes
75 g (3 oz) sesame seeds
60 ml (2½ fl oz) tahini*

● In a medium saucepan melt the chocolate, butter and liquid glucose, stirring gently over a low heat. Be careful not to burn the chocolate.

● Meanwhile, measure out the Rice Crispies, cornflakes and sesame seeds in a large bowl. Once the butter and chocolate mixture is nicely melted, add the tahini and mix through. Now combine this with the cereal and sesame seeds, mixing well to make sure all the cereal is coated.

● Line some mini muffin tins with paper cases. Using two spoons, spoon the mixture into the paper cases. Leave to cool in the fridge for a minimum of 2 hours before serving.

 *IF YOU HAVEN'T GOT TAHINI, TRY USING PEANUT BUTTER. CRUNCHY OR SMOOTH WILL DO THE JOB.

 THESE ARE GREAT FOR PARTIES OR AS LUNCH BOX TREATS. THEY WILL KEEP IN THE FRIDGE IN AN AIRTIGHT CONTAINER FOR AT LEAST A WEEK, ALTHOUGH I THINK YOU'LL FIND THAT THEY WILL DISAPPEAR QUITE QUICKLY.

Gingerbread People

This is a great recipe to make with kids as it's very forgiving. Clear some space and let them get stuck in. Alternatively, bake them as blanks and then let the children decorate them with coloured icing.

350 g (11½ oz) gluten-free plain flour
2 tsp ground ginger
1 tsp bicarbonate of soda
100 g (4 oz) cold butter, diced
100 g (4 oz) dark brown sugar

75 g (3 oz) caster sugar
1 egg
4 tbsp honey
Raisins
Glacé cherries
Decorating icing

● Pre-heat the oven to 190°C (375°F) Gas 5. Lightly grease a baking sheet.

● Sift the flour into a large bowl. Add the ginger and bicarbonate of soda. Rub the butter into the flour mixture until it resembles coarse breadcrumbs. Add the sugars, egg and honey and blend to make a soft dough. If the dough appears to be too wet, add a little more flour. If too dry, add a few drops of water or a little more egg.

● Knead the dough until smooth on a lightly floured surface. Roll it out as evenly as possible to a thickness of 5 mm (¼ in).

● Using shaped cookie cutters, cut out gingerbread shapes and carefully place on the baking sheet. Decorate with raisins and cherries.

● Bake for about 12 minutes until just lightly brown. Leave to cool

LUNCHBOX IDEA

for a few minutes before lifting them carefully on to a wire rack to cool. Decorate with tubes of icing. Store in an airtight tin for about 2–3 days. You can also freeze them.

Gingerbread

Iced Sugar Cookies (MAKES ABOUT 50 COOKIES)

These are great for children's parties. Get the children involved and let them have fun using cookie cutters and ready-made icing to make their own designs.

150 g (5 oz) gluten-free plain flour
100 g (4 oz) ground almonds
1½ tsp gluten-free baking powder
½ tsp bicarbonate of soda
85 g (3½ oz) unsalted butter

200 g (7 oz) caster sugar
1 egg
1 tsp vanilla extract
Decorating icing

● Combine the flour, almonds, baking powder and bicarbonate of soda in a bowl. In a separate bowl cream the butter and sugar until light and fluffy. Add the egg and vanilla and beat well.

● Gently add the flour mixture to make a stiff dough. Add a little more flour if necessary. Divide the dough in half and shape each half into a rectangle. Flatten out slightly with a rolling pin. Wrap in clingfilm and chill for a minimum of 2 hours. You can keep the dough in the freezer for about a month.

To prepare cookies

● Pre-heat the oven to 190°C (375°F) Gas 5.

● Lightly dust the work surface with flour. Roll out the dough to 3 mm (⅛ in) thickness. Cut out the cookies with decorative cutters and place on an ungreased baking sheet. If the dough gets too soft, place back in the freezer to firm up a little before continuing.

● Leave plenty of space between the cookies on the baking

GREAT ACTIVITY FOR PARTIES

sheet as they will spread. Bake for 8–10 minutes until lightly golden around the edges. Leave to cool on the baking sheet for a few minutes before transferring to a wire rack. Allow to cool completely before decorating with tubes of writing icing.

Note: These cookies are best within 1–2 days of being made. You can store them in an airtight container.

Iced cookies

MENU PLANNER

Magic Monday Night Supper

Polenta and Cumin Pork Chops
(page 137)
Carrots á la Ewelme (page 157)
Mashed Potatoes
Chocolate and Vanilla Swirly
Puddings (page 172)

Tuesday Tasty Indian Takeaway

Chicken and Vegetable Curry
(page 138)
Basmati Rice
Tropical Rice Crispy Bars
(page 187)

Wednesday Wizzy Busy Supper

Nan's Seafood Pot (page 147)
Brown Rice
Chocolate Truffle Cookies
(page 177)

Thursday's Oriental Express

Kung Po Prawn Stir Fry
(page 149)
Plain Rice
Brownies (page 180)

Friday Fish 'n' Chip Supper

Fish Fingers or Crispy Chicken
Nuggets (pages 60 or 56)
Oven Chips or Polenta Chips
(page 64)
Soft Cheese Herb Dip
(page 195)
Fruity Mousse (page 175)

Saturday Fusion Fiesta
Chicken Kebabs with Peanut
Sauce (page 144)
Torta de Mazorca (page 150)
Dalia's Luscious Lemon Bars
(page 184)

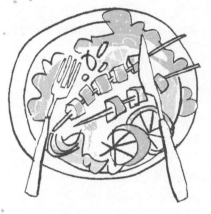

Happy Home Sunday Lunch
Chicken Pot Pie (page 140)
Steamed Vegetables
Apple and Rhubarb
Crumble (page 174)

Chihuahua Night
Enchilada Pie (page 142)
Green Salad
Chocolate Roulade (page 206)

Sports Candy Night
Vegetable Bake (page 151)
Roast Tomato Sauce (page 134)
Green Salad
Peanut Butter Cookies
(page 178)

Cookies

MENU PLANNER

Party Menu Planner

Menu 1 (Suitable for young childen)
Breadsticks (page 200)
Soft Cheese Herb Dip (page 195)
Guacamole Dip (page 196)
Crudités
Crispy Chicken Nuggets (page 56)
Polenta Chips (page 64)
Plate of cold meats including turkey, salami, ham, cheese
Lovely Little Cupcakes (page 198)

Menu 2 (Suitable for older children)
Quick Pizza (page 66) or Tacos (page 125)
Chocolate Truffle Cookies (page 177)
Ice Cream Sundaes (page 72)

Menu 3 (A more substantial menu for christening, anniversaries, etc)
Chicken, Apricot and Pine Nut Salad (page 123)
Deborah's Delicious Meatballs (page 58)
Torta de Mazorca (page 150)
Nan's Chopped Salad (page 122)
Brenda's Lemon Meringue Ice Cream Cake (page 201)
Brownies (page 180)

Menu 4 (Easy and informal)

Prairie Mix (page 197)
Four Layer Latin Dip (page 194)
Corn Tortillas
Gluten–free Crisps
Guacamole Dip (page 196)
Crudités
Gluten–free sausages or chicken drumsticks
Crazy Crunchy Cakes (page 209)

Dips
↓ here

smoothie

WEBSITES

Useful Websites and Specialist Suppliers

Coeliac Disease Help and Advice

Coeliac UK
3rd Floor, Apollo Centre
Desborough Road
High Wycombe
Bucks HP11 2QW
Telephone: 01494 437278
www.coeliac.org.uk

Celiac Disease Foundation
For further information
regarding coeliac disease in
the USA visit www.celiac.org

The Coeliac Society
For further information
regarding coeliac disease
in Australia visit
www.coeliac.org.au.

Coeliac Society of New Zealand
For New Zealand visit
www.coeliac.co.nz.

Gluten-free passport
Travel advice and useful
translations in several
languages for key phrases.
www.glutenfreepassport.com

Specialist Suppliers

Goodness Direct
South March
Daventry
Northants NN11 4PH
www.goodnessdirect.co.uk

Lifestyle Health Care Ltd
Centenary Business Park
Henley-on-Thames
Oxfordshire RG9 1DS
www.gfdiet.com

The Cool Chile Company
www.coolchile.co.uk

gluten-free cookbook FOR KIDS

Index

Acknowledgements

Thank you Marc for all your help during the writing of this book. It could not have happened without your love and support. Thank you to Ruthie and Lucia for being so patient and allowing mummy time off to get this done. You've earned lots of stars! Thank you to all my wonderful recipe testers, including Nanci Austin, Julia Dionian, Sarah Fishburn, Deborah Lambert, Miranda Robinson and Brenda Welch.

Thank you to Janet and Allen Spence for doing such a fantastic job of looking after Lucia and keeping her entertained. Thank you to Sam Royal for helping to keep the place tidy! Thank you to Yury, Marina, Anastasia and Alexey for doing more than your share of school runs.

Thank you to all my friends and family who have made such wonderful recipe contributions. I am eternally grateful. Special thanks to the Abuelas Barbara and Jeanine and to Tia Sophie and Aunt Ruthie.

Thank you to the staff at Vermillion who made this book possible. In particular, thank you to Miranda West for shepherding this project and for being such a great champion.

Thank you to David and Michael Charles, Rosie, Cameron and Heather Fishburn and Todd and Sean Robinson for being such fantastic guinea pigs.

Author Biography

Adriana Rabinovich grew up in Colombia, then moved to the US before coming to Britain. After a career in design and advertising she set up her own business, The Little Red Barn.

The Little Red Barn had a prestigious customer list selling the most sought after brownies, biscotti and cookies in the UK. Harvey Nichols, Selfridges, Fortnum & Mason and Starbucks stocked her products and it is rumoured that her dedicated fan base included the inhabitants of Number 10 Downing Street. *The Little Red Barn Baking Book* was published by Ebury Press in 2000.

Adriana sold her company prior to her daughter Ruth's arrival. Ruth was diagnosed with Coeliac Disease in 2004 and since then Adriana has become an expert on gluten-free cooking. Her aim is to make delicious gluten-free cooking and baking widely accessible.

Adriana lives in Oxfordshire with her husband Marc and their two daughters, Ruth and Lucia.

Please visit us at: www.glutenfree4kids.com